"Rabbi John Rosove has given a gift to all of us who care about engaging the next generation in Jewish life. The letters to his sons are really love-letters from countless voices of Jewish wisdom across history to all those young people who are seeking purpose in their lives. From wrestling with God to advocating for peace and justice in Israel and at home and living a life of purpose, this book is a compelling case for the joy of being Jewish."

—**Rabbi Jonah Pesner**, is the Director of the Religious Action Center of Reform Judaism in Washington, D.C., and is Senior Vice President of the Union for Reform Judaism. Named one of the most influential rabbis in America by *Newsweek* magazine, he is an inspirational leader, creative entrepreneur, and tireless advocate for social justice.

"Rabbi Rosove has written a wonderful book, a love letter to his children, and through them, to all our children. Prodigiously knowledgeable, exceedingly wise, and refreshingly honest, Rabbi Rosove has described why Judaism matters. It should serve as a touching testament of faith, spanning the generations for generations to come."

—**Rabbi Ammiel Hirsch** is Senior Rabbi of Stephen Wise Free Synagogue, New York City, and is the co-author of *One People, Two Worlds: A Reform rabbi and an Orthodox rabbi explore the issues that divide them* with Rabbi Yaakov Yosef Reinman.

"John Rosove's letters to his sons based on his life, philosophy, and rabbinic work address what it means to be a liberal and ethical Jew and a lover of Israel in an era when none are automatic. He writes in an unassuming personal style steeped in traditional texts as he confronts conflicts of faith and objectivity, Zionist pride and loving criticism of the Jewish state, traditional observance, and religious innovation. He is never gratuitous and invites his readers into his family conversation because what he says is applicable to us all."

—**Susan Freudenheim** is the Executive Director of Jewish World Watch, was formerly the Managing Editor of the *Los Angeles Jewish Journal* and an editor at the *Los Angeles Times*.

T0161733

PRAISE FOR

WHY JUDAISM MATTERS

"John Rosove does what so many of us have struggled to do, and does it brilliantly: He makes the case for liberal Judaism to his children. As Rosove shows, liberal Judaism is choice-driven, messy, and always evolving, "traditional" in some ways and "radical" in others. It is also optimistic, spiritual, and progressive in both personal and political ethics. Without avoiding the hard stuff, such as intermarriage and Israel, Rabbi Rosove weaves all of these strands together to show the deep satisfactions of living and believing as a liberal Jew. All serious Jews, liberal or otherwise, should read this book."

—**Rabbi Eric H. Yoffie** is President Emeritus of the Union for Reform Judaism and a regular columnist for the Israeli daily newspaper *Haaretz*.

"Rabbi John Rosove addresses his intellectual and well-reasoned investigation of faith to his own sons, which sets this book apart for its candor and its ability to penetrate not only the mind but also the heart."

—**Matthew Weiner** is a writer, director, producer, and the creator of the AMC television drama series *Mad Men*, and he is noted for his work as a writer and producer on the HBO drama series *The Sopranos*. Matthew has received nine Primetime Emmy Awards.

"Rabbi John Rosove has written a book of the utmost importance for our time. It is an imperative read for all those who struggle with the changing and evolving attitudes towards belonging, behavior, and belief. His analysis, stemming from deeply personal contemplation and decades of rabbinic experience, offers clear yet sophisticated approaches to tackling the challenges facing this generation and those to come. This book offers a treasure of wisdom through the lens of Jewish texts—both ancient and modern—which help to frame life's major issues, taking the reader from the particular to the universal. Israel is one of the most complicated of issues tackled in this volume and his chapter on Israel bridges the divide between Israel's critics and staunch supporters, offering a comforting approach to those who are deeply at odds with Israel and offers an important opportunity for a shift in our basic narrative. Moving beyond the conversation of crisis is critical for the millennial generation."

—**Rabbi Josh Weinberg** is President of the Association of Reform Zionists of America and is a leading young voice in world-wide Zionist politics and affairs.

"Rabbi John Rosove gets it. Here is a religious leader not afraid to tell it like it is, encapsulating for his audience the profound disaffection so many young Jews feel toward their heritage. But instead of letting them walk away, he makes a powerful case for the relevance of tradition in creating meaningful lives. In our technology-saturated, attention-absorbing age, Rosove offers religion-as-reprieve, his fresh vision of a thoroughly modern, politically-engaged and inclusive Judaism."

—**Danielle Berrin** is a columnist and cover-story journalist for the *Los Angeles Jewish Journal*. She is known for her *Hollywood Jew* blog, has appeared as a commentator on CNN and MSNBC, and published work for *The Guardian*, *British Esquire*, and *The Atlantic*.

"Rabbi Rosove's letters to his sons are full of Talmudic tales and practical parables, ancient wisdom with modern relevance, spiritual comfort, and intellectual provocation. Whether his subject is faith, love, intermarriage, success, Jewish continuity, or the creation of a meaningful legacy, you'll find yourself quoting lines from this beautiful book long after you've reached its final blessing."

—**Letty Cottin Pogrebin** is a writer, speaker, social justice activist, and author of eleven books including *Deborah, Golda, and Me: Being Female & Jewish in America* and *Single Jewish Male Seeking Soul Mate*. She is also a founding editor of *Ms. Magazine*, is a regular columnist for *Moment Magazine*, and has written op-eds in *The New York Times*, *Washington Post*, *Huffington Post*, *Boston Globe*, *Philadelphia Inquirer, L.A. Times, Toronto Star, The Nation, Harpers Bazaar, Travel & Leisure, Family Circle,* and *Good Housekeeping*.

"If you're a fellow Reform millennial, give yourself the gift of John's insights. This book is written in a breezy, gentle, readable style that is welcoming without losing sharp insight. It makes an even better case for Judaism than challah. It was so enjoyable and refreshing to read and persuasive without ever being pushy. Rosove managed to do what only a truly worthy slice of kugel or chance viewing of *Fiddler* has done for me: reactivate my sense of wonder and gratitude about being Jewish. I am a huge *WJM* fan."

—**Jen Spyra** is a staff comedy writer on *The Late Show with Stephen Colbert* (CBS) and formerly was a senior writer for *The Onion*. Her writing has appeared in *The New Yorker, McSweeney's, The Wall Street Journal, The New York Daily News,* and *The Daily Beast,* and she has been featured by The Laugh Factory, Chicago's Best Standup Show Case.

WHY JUDAISM MATTERS

LETTERS OF A LIBERAL RABBI
TO HIS CHILDREN AND THE
MILLENNIAL GENERATION

RABBI JOHN L. ROSOVE
AFTERWORD BY DANIEL AND DAVID ROSOVE

For People of All Faiths, All Backgrounds
JEWISH LIGHTS Publishing
Nashville, Tennessee

Jewish Lights Publishing
an imprint of Turner Publishing Company
Nashville, Tennessee
New York, New York
www.jewishlights.com
www.turnerpublishing.com

Why Judaism Matters:
Letters of a Liberal Rabbi to His Children and the Millennial Generation

All rights reserved. No part of this book may be reproduced or transmitted in any form or by any means, electronic or mechanical, including photocopying, recording, or by any information storage and retrieval system, without permission in writing from the publisher.

For information regarding permission to reprint material from this book, please mail or fax your request in writing to Jewish Lights Publishing, Permission Department, at the address / fax number listed below, or email your request to submissions@turnerpublishing.com.

© 2017 by John L. Rosove

A note on translations and gender-inclusive language for God: Unless otherwise indicated, all translations of the Hebrew Bible are taken from the Jewish Publication Society (JPS) version and those from the Talmud are taken from the Soncino edition. I refer to the God of Israel as "God," "Adonai," or "YHVH." I have replaced gender-exclusive pronouns for God (he, his, etc.) with Creator, Almighty, and the One, etc.

Library of Congress Cataloging-in-Publication Data
Names: Rosove, John L., author.
Title: Why Judaism matters : letters of a liberal rabbi to his children and
  the millennial generation / Rabbi John L. Rosove ; afterword by Daniel and
  David Rosove.
Description: Nashville, Tennessee : Jewish Lights, [2017] | Includes
  bibliographical references.
Identifiers: LCCN 2017033298 | ISBN 9781683367055 (pbk.)
Subjects: LCSH: Reform Judaism.
Classification: LCC BM197 .R65 2017 | DDC 296.8/341--dc23
LC record available at https://lccn.loc.gov/2017033298

Cover design: Maddie Cothren
Interior design: Tim Holtz

Printed in the United States of America
17 18 19 20 9 8 7 6 5 4 3 2 1

For Daniel and David
In gratitude to Barbara

Content

Why Being Jewish Matters

Dear Daniel and David:

Once, having a rabbi for a father would have sealed your fate, and you would have been pushed to follow my path and become rabbis too. But we practice liberal Judaism, and our family is nontraditional and Western educated, so your mother and I have always encouraged you to choose your own course and find your own relationship to Judaism and the Jewish people.

With no pressure from me or our community to conform to set expectations or ritual standards, you are each free to come to your own way of living a meaningful Jewish life. You could take the radical path, as many people do, and turn away from the synagogue, Jewish tradition, the Jewish community, and everything associated with it. Many of your peers have done so and are Jewish in name only. To them our traditions and teachings seem archaic or irrelevant, and they don't recognize how much of their cultural identity, tastes, values, and proclivities that feel like "home" to them are woven generally into the greater fabric of Judaism in which they have grown up, and into liberal Judaism in particular.

They assume that our religion is rooted in plagues and a belief in a wrathful God who deals in the black and white of good and evil. They see the Jewish people as traumatized by persecution, and our rituals, faith, and way of being in the world as from another era, from long ago. They can't see the point of continuing it, or its relevance to their lives.

They may feel Jewish in their guts, and they may even know a bit of Yiddish, such as "kishkes," "chutzpah," and "putz," to throw into conversation, but they don't see a way for them to get a toehold in the Jewish community and modern Jewish life. So they don't. They drift away from their synagogue, if they were ever part of one to begin with. And when they fall in love with someone who is not Jewish, as 50 to 60 percent of young American Jews do today, they drop their struggle to understand Jewish tradition or to maintain their connections to Judaism and the Jewish community and simply let it all go. When their elders wail and worry whether they will have Jewish grandchildren, they don't quite know what the fuss is all about. They hardly know how to explain to their non-Jewish partners and children what our tradition values most and how it has shaped us as a people. They don't hold on to their Jewishness, much less pass it on to their kids, because they feel as though they have always been on the outside, not tethered the way their grandparents and great-grandparents were in more traditional communities.

Many are also turned off by a growing separatism and extremism in the Jewish community, by a trend toward exclusionary tribalism and fierce self-righteous nationalism, by an intolerant orthodoxy that they not only don't like but also can't understand. They'd rather identify with what they believe is the Jewish ethical tradition and our people's universal impulse, without doing anything particularly Jewish, and say that's enough to identify as Jews. They skip any ritual or observances and feel no particular loyalty to Jews, the Jewish people, and the State of Israel. They consider keeping kosher or celebrating Shabbat not necessarily as wrong but as a sign of being narrow in their lifestyle. They distrust extremism of all kinds, particularly Jewish extremism. They throw their hands up, turn away completely, and never look back.

But in doing so, I believe they're not seeing what Jewish tradition is or could be. If only they knew how many reasons they have to stay. The best of liberal Western tradition embodies many of the same values that we American liberal Jews hold dear. Our country has been shaped in part by the wisdom of the biblical prophets and reflects the compassion of rabbinic tradition. There are so many compelling reasons to make the effort to discover these connections, synthesize it all, and maintain a Jewish identity.

Let me be very specific about the issue that's at the core of all my letters to you guys in one way or another. The question I want each of you to ask yourself is: "Why stay Jewish?" I'd like to make the case that to identify as a liberal Jew in America today is to connect with a deeply intellectual, skeptical, activistic, and optimistic tradition that has at its core a nuanced spirituality, strong ethical roots, and clarity of values, all of which can help us make our lives more meaningful. Embracing that liberal Jewish identity is often the answer to the very question that I asked myself, when I was young and throughout all my years, and that I know you both have asked yourselves since you were very young: "How can I live as my fullest self?" We all grapple with that question as we move through life. It seems tragic to me and a huge missed opportunity that so many Jews, especially among your peers, turn away from something that may suit them so perfectly—without knowing how right it is for them.

Knowing you both as I do, I'm confident that you'll maintain your connection to Judaism and Jewish liberal values as you continue to build your lives outside our home. Your dad is a rabbi after all. But I know that even you may have difficulty explaining to outsiders the liberal Jewish essence that can appear to be merely a loose conglomeration of belief, ethics, history, tradition, politics, poetry, social activism, and progressive Zionism. It's complicated to tie all the threads of what makes us Americans, liberals, and Jews together in a way that's meaningful and grounded in this time and place.

So in these letters I hope to offer you a starting point for thinking and talking about those essential threads that make us the liberal Jews we are and that tie us to the very best of Jewish tradition. I'll think out loud to you and tell you how I came to the understandings I have now. I'll pull out some of the wisdom I've learned from my study of our ancient holy books, from my teachers, from some of the greatest Jewish leaders and thinkers over the centuries, and from my own life experience, including my engagement in social justice work and my progressive Israel and Zionist activism. So much of the wisdom I've learned is very old, going back hundreds and even thousands of years; amazingly, it still resonates strongly today as each of us struggles to find meaning, purpose, and direction. I want to share what has most moved and helped me and what I leaned on for inspiration when I was your age, struggling perhaps in some of the same ways you are now. I hope that these letters will be meaningful to you.

I hope to help weave these various threads together, and I know you'll combine them in ways that are as individual as you are. That's as it should be. The way I live as a Jew can't be the way you do, because you are different from me. You are finding your way as young adults in a time that sometimes barely resembles the one in which I grew up. But I hope you'll each pick up many of these threads, ponder them, and most of all weave them into your life actively, in your own way. These common themes, ideas, and ways of thinking about and being in the world connect you to an unbroken tradition that is your heritage, your cultural genome, your values, and Judaism's profound gift to you. And when you have children of your own, I hope that these letters will help you pass that gift to them.

Love,
Dad

Part I

The Essence of Liberal Judaism

You Don't Have to Believe
in God to Be a Jew

Dear Daniel and David:

I want to start by putting a big, difficult, and divisive topic on the table: God.

In many religions, and in some Jewish communities, "Do you believe in God?" is a threshold question. Answer yes and you are one of the fold. Answer no and you have a problem.

So it is with reticence or a mildly defiant tone that many Jews tell me, "Rabbi, I don't believe in God." I sometimes think that on some level they expect someone—that is, me—to hear that statement and "cast them out."

The conversation gets interesting if we talk about the nature of the God they find so incredible. Often it turns out to be the white-haired figure touching fingers with Adam on the Sistine Chapel ceiling—the commanding, rewarding, and punishing God of the High Holy Day prayer book.

The fact is, most modern liberal Jews today don't rationally accept the notion of such a God, especially given the fact that all around us innocent people do suffer and the all-knowing, all-powerful, all-good God of tradition either ignores them or doesn't exist.

When people tell me that they don't believe in God—either because they have seen no empirical evidence that God exists or because they can't rationally accept the God of the Bible and of the medieval rabbis—I understand completely. I don't believe in that God either.

I say this as one who has spent decades thinking about God, faith, and the insights and truths Jewish tradition offers us. I've studied Torah seriously for more than forty years and considered the spiritual gifts of some of our greatest thinkers, mystics, and poets. I see clearly that we live in a vastly different world from that of our ancestors, whose ideas of God evolved from the social models that surrounded them—the world of feudal kings and vassals.

Modernity, which emphasizes the uniqueness of the individual, free from the shackles of convention and tradition, has produced very different kinds of Jews, some of whom traditional Judaism wouldn't recognize as particularly Jewish at all.

One says, "I'm a religious person in that I feel a connection to something eternal and infinite that's in my soul and in yours. But I don't believe in a personal God, and all this talk about God as king and me as servant is meaningless to me."

Another says, "I'm grateful for the gifts of health, meaningful work, and love. Sometimes I feel overwhelmed by gratitude and a sense of inadequacy to express how blessed I feel, and that's about as close as I come to prayer. But that prayer is addressed to life itself—to no one in particular, and surely not to 'God.'"

Many Jews with spiritual yearnings share these sentiments and orientations. But too often they don't bother to look for a spiritual home within the Jewish community because they assume they won't find one there, or that they won't be touched or engaged on the level of soul.

What I'd like to tell you—and them—is that we can all share in this search and satisfy the deep yearnings of our spirits by pulling inspiration from both modern life and the mystical traditions of Judaism, which speak about God not in terms of thunderbolts but rather as an inner spark. The question that's most pertinent to us now isn't "Do you believe in God?" Rather, it's "How do I—and how can I—experience myself as a spiritual being?"

A search that starts with that question turns our focus to the stirrings of our own intuition and experience and doesn't ask us to marshal empirical evidence that some God-force exists outside us. When our search is an interior one, it's possible to say that we are spiritual beings without having to affirm, deny, or concern ourselves with belief in God at all. We open ourselves to awe, wonder, and gratitude, and in the vastness of all of that, we connect with our souls and the ancient mysteries threaded through our modern lives.

Here's a small example of what I'm talking about. On September 5, 1977, when I was your age, NASA launched a small 1,590-pound spacecraft called *Voyager 1*. The mission's purpose was to study the outer solar system and beyond.

The small craft carried both observational equipment and messages intended for any future finders: a golden record of greetings in fifty languages, including one whale language; a twelve-minute sound essay that included a kiss, a baby's cry, and the meditations of a young woman in love; 116 encoded pictures meant to show our science, our civilization, and ourselves; and ninety minutes of Earth's greatest hits, Eastern and Western, classical and folk, including a Navajo night chant, a Pygmy girl's initiation song, a Peruvian wedding song, compositions from some of our great composers (Bach, Beethoven, Mozart, Stravinsky), a selection from Louis Armstrong, and Chuck Berry's "Johnny B. Goode." If by some infinitesimally slight chance sentient beings intercepted the craft at some point in its travels, these artifacts of our civilization were meant to give them an idea of who we were, the occupants of planet Earth in the Milky Way galaxy in this era.

I got my best sense of this mission and the scale of its aspirations when my brother, your Uncle Michael, sent me an eight-minute video written and narrated by the astronomer and astrophysicist Carl Sagan for his 1980 television series *Cosmos: A Personal Voyage*. Sagan described *Voyager 1* and its twin, *Voyager 2*, which had been launched a month earlier. Here is that description, as found in Sagan's book *Pale Blue Dot*:

> The *Voyager* spacecraft ... barreling along at almost a million miles a day ... will not leave the solar system for hundreds of centuries....
> Then, at last ... broken free of the gravitational shackles that once bound them to the sun, the *Voyagers* will make for the open sea of interstellar space....
>
> The spacecraft will wander for ages in the calm, cold interstellar blackness—where there is almost nothing to erode them. Once out of the solar system, they will remain intact for a billion years or more as they circumnavigate the center of the Milky Way galaxy....
>
> In five billion years, all humans will have become extinct or evolved into other beings, none of our artifacts will have survived on

> Earth ... and the evolution of the sun will have burned the Earth into
> a crisp or reduced it to a whirl of atoms.
>
> Far from home, untouched by these remote events, the *Voyagers*,
> bearing the memories of a world that is no more, will fly on.[1]

Imagine a human-made object filled with recorded memory traveling through interstellar space ... forever.

How are we supposed to wrap our minds around such a phenomenon, except to be struck dumb in awe and amazement?

The wonder I still feel doesn't require any sort of belief in a God-figure pulling the *Voyagers* through space. And the part of me that's so moved by the wonder and poetry of life—I'd call this part the soul—doesn't require grandeur on a *Voyager* scale to be awakened, I've realized.

These days I seem to experience this wonder frequently—when walking in my neighborhood; reading something beautifully written; hearing magnificent music; spending time with Mom and you guys; communing sweetly with Sasha [our little white Coton de Tulear dog]; and sitting quietly on our deck above the treetops, drinking red wine in the late afternoon, feeling the breeze on my face, and hearing the rustling of leaves.

Over the years I've found that my capacity to experience awe and wonder has grown in direct proportion to how grateful I feel for the gifts in my life. It's the mystics' God, the God of inwardness, that expands us in this way and allows us to tap the hidden spiritual waters inside us.

The truth taught by the mystics is that the individual isn't separate from God. God is the mystery within us, inside every soul, in the sparks of light hidden beneath the shards, in the love that inspires generosity and compassion.

Rebbe Nachman of Breslov teaches that the divine presence is flowing constantly into the world as the light of awareness, but an inner vessel needs to be created within every human being so that the light might be received. A vessel is made whenever a heart opens to give love to others. This is one meaning of the verse *Asu li mikdash v'shachanti b'tocham*, "Make for me a sanctuary that I may dwell within them" (Exodus 25:8, my translation). The literal translation of *b'tocham* is "within them," suggesting that God is within each human being. Each of us is called upon to be a holy vessel, dispensing divine light and love.

This mystical experience of godlikeness not only revitalizes us, but it also breaks down unnecessary barriers between people generally and between Jews specifically. It enables us to have a far more inclusive and expansive vision of Jewish life and humankind as a whole. Reaching across distinctions, it inspires the understanding that divinity flows in infinite variety, shines everywhere through a rainbow of light, and flows into a coat of many colors that correspond to diverse peoples, cultures, and individual beings throughout the world.

Here's what I'd like you to know: Every peak emotional moment of joy, appreciation, and gratitude is similar in kind to the classic religious and prophetic moments recorded in the great books of Jewish literature, and every spiritual moment we have is a revelation of some deeper truth. Recognizing that, as we contemplate the depths of space or each other's eyes, we can be reminded that we are part of something far greater than ourselves.

All great spiritual insight begins inside us and flows outward. The problem with our traditional liturgy is that too often it doesn't seem to reflect this perspective. It's frequently heavy-handed and at times suffocating. Though I value much of it for its hidden truths and place in our history and tradition, I've learned to transcend some of the language and metaphor, and to turn the imagery around so I can think and react differently. In this way I embrace the deeper and sustaining message at the heart and soul of Judaism.

The metaphor of godliness hidden in every soul is hardly new to Jewish tradition, but it's new and revolutionary to many of us. Modernity, for all its benefits, has tended to reject the teachings of the great Jewish mystics because their writings and teachings carried people into nonrational, nonlinear, intuitive thinking, and such thinking was contrary to the rationalism that characterized the Enlightenment.

But now we're hungry for the spiritual answers that our linear, rational minds can't deliver—and the embracing sense of community that spiritual openness can help create.

Rabbi Abraham Joshua Heschel, who is among our people's greatest poets of the soul, describes what the spiritual experience is all about:

> Our radical amazement responds to the mystery, but does not produce it. You and I have not invented the grandeur of the sky nor

endowed the human being with the mystery of birth and death. We
do not create the ineffable, we encounter it…. The awareness of the
ineffable is that with which our search must begin…. The search
of reason ends at the shore of the known; on the immense expanse
beyond it only the sense of the ineffable can glide; … reason cannot
go beyond the shore, and the sense of the ineffable is out of place
where we measure, where we weigh.[2]

Jewish tradition does many things, and two of the most important are that
it feeds the mind and inspires the soul. I don't think we need to put aside
our left-brain training as we open ourselves to what the mystics can teach
us. Rather, we can ask the questions that will bring us greater awareness
of our souls. In every aspect of your life, I want each of you to ask yourself, "How can I connect to what's eternal and infinite within me and the
world? How can I connect with a sense of awe and wonder on the one
hand and gratitude for the fact of existence and my capacity to feel it at all
on the other?"

This search, whether we use the word "God" or not, pulls us into
the deep and vital current of Judaism. It doesn't demand that the atheists
and agnostics among us suspend their doubts and disbelief. It doesn't ask
you to slink away if you don't believe in God. Instead, it asks all of us to
become more aware of the musings of our right-brain intuition, and to
think about the spiritual significance of our hours and days, the mun-
danities and the milestones of our lives, such as falling in love; attending
weddings, births, b'nai mitzvah celebrations, conversions, and anniversa-
ries; being part of our family gatherings; spending time alone; creating art,
film, music, literature, poetry, dance, and architecture; doing good works
in the community; and reaching out to people in need.

We don't need to believe in a plague- and miracle-wielding God outside us to be Jews and spiritual beings. Our task instead is to be more than
secular actors in our human drama as it unfolds, to understand that we
aren't just separate, willful beings making our way in a chaotic, meaningless existence. We also each have a unique glow of light in our souls—the
beautiful, inexplicable, and awe-inspiring spark of life. It's by seeing the
light in one another and then drawing our separate lights together into
a larger glow that we discover and understand the deeper truth about
ourselves, each other, and the world. We begin to see that it may be true,

as one Hasidic sage once noted, that "the human being is the language of God," because God is present in each of our souls.[3] We each long to know the Source from which we come and to which we return.

Whether we speak of that Source as God or Nature or Life or Love, we and the mystics and the scientists are all talking about the same thing, and Judaism is embracing enough to welcome us all.

Love,
Dad

Why Religion Still Has Value

Dear Daniel and David:

I often hear people say that the world would be a better, more peaceful place if we simply got rid of religion. Hate, tension, discord, racism, anti-Semitism, Islamophobia, sexism, misogyny, homophobia, violence— all these ills sometimes seem rooted in various sects' interpretations of their holy books and their insistence that theirs is the only truth.

I understand how easy it is to see Judaism in this light. Our fundamental statement of faith is the Sh'ma: *Sh'ma Yisrael, YHVH, Eloheinu, YHVH Echad*, "Listen, O Israel, YHVH is our God, YHVH is One" (Deuteronomy 6:4). This statement, which traditional Jews say three times a day in prayer and we all say when we take the Torah from the holy ark, asserts that God's unity is the first and primary principle in Judaism. This belief is at the core of all three monotheistic faiths: Judaism, Christianity, and Islam.

But it's a grave misunderstanding to think "YHVH is One" means "our God is the only God" or "our way is the only way." As British philosopher and scholar Rabbi Jonathan Sacks explains in his book *The Dignity of Difference*,

> Biblical monotheism is not the idea that there is one God and therefore one gateway to His presence. To the contrary, it is the idea that the unity of God is to be found in the diversity of creation. This applies to the natural world. What is real and the proper object of our wonder is not the Platonic form of a leaf but the 250,000 different kinds there actually are; not the quintessential bird but the 9,000 species that

exist today; not the metalanguage that embraces all others, but the 6,000 languages still spoken throughout the world. Thanks to our newfound knowledge of DNA we now know that all life in its astonishing complexity had a single origin.[1]

This is similar to what I call the Unity principle which understands the world as interconnected, with a common breath, a common spark, linking the vast diversity of life—all people and things, physical and spiritual. This understanding has guided me in my relationships with family and friends, with colleagues and congregants, and with every stranger I encounter. It shapes my approach to interfaith and intergroup work, liberal politics, social justice activism, and progressive Zionism.

Whether you think in terms of God or science, the Unity principle holds—even scientists believe that the universe has a common origin and a singular beginning point and that the laws of physics unite the physical world. We can't escape our interconnectedness.

Nor can we separate the love of God—the creative and constructive force of life in the universe—from the love between human beings. They're two sides of the same coin. In revering and honoring God, or life, we necessarily revere and honor each other.

These two verses from the Torah are closely tied: "Love your fellow as yourself" (Leviticus 19:18) and "Love [Adonai] your God with all your heart and with all your soul and with all your might" (Deuteronomy 6:5).[2] Our love for each other and for God (or life) are ineffable, beyond reason. They are emanations of the heart and soul. When two people join together in love, God abides there too. As theologian Martin Buber taught, in our love for our fellow we shall find God. God, he explained, is in the "in-betweenness" (*Zwischeninstanz*) of relationships.[3]

There are, of course, many different kinds of love. Mom and I love each other differently from the way we love you. You love each other as brothers differently from the way you love us, your friends, and your romantic partners. All these loves are different from the love you feel for your teachers and mentors, peers and coworkers, or our dog, Sasha. They are different from the love with which you embrace art, music, film, dance, sports, literature, and ideas.

But present in all these kinds of love is our yearning to connect to—and *belong* to—something greater than ourselves. When we acknowledge the Unity principle, we belong to everyone else, and everyone else belongs to us, regardless of race, religion, gender, sexual orientation, ethnicity, or nationality. Belonging means that we are accountable to and responsible for the well-being of every other person. This isn't just an ethical truth; it is also the fundamental Jewish religious principle at the core of our tradition.

This is stated in a more limited way in the Talmud: *Kol Yisrael areivim zeh bazeh*, "All Israel is responsible for each other" (*Shavuot* 39a). We interpret this to mean that all Jews, no matter where we live in the world, are connected and responsible for one another's safety and well-being. *Ahavat Yisrael*, love of Israel, is a high Jewish value.

Yet though we are part of a tribal system, we are far more than a tribe. The Passover Haggadah reminds us of our connections to others, and even to our enemies, as shown in a famous rabbinic legend. The Egyptians are drowned in the Sea of Reeds, but God suffers when even the enemies of God's people perish. We're taught that the suffering and death of any human being ought to be a source of sadness for everyone. That's the understanding behind the part of the Seder ritual in which we read the ten plagues and reduce the wine in our cups by one drop for each plague. The wine is a symbol of our joy at our liberation from bondage, and anytime others experience suffering, the totality of our joy must diminish.

Fighting the Duality That Distorts Us

This sense of empathy, of humanity as a unified whole, is strongly challenged by what Rabbi Sacks calls "pathological dualism," which casts out and fears the other. He sees the thread of this dualism running through the murderous ideologies of fundamentalist extremists in Judaism, Christianity, and Islam, and describes it as a distortion of the pure monotheism that distinguishes our three great monotheistic religions. Rabbi Sacks writes:

> Pathological dualism does three things. It makes you dehumanize and demonize your enemies. It leads you to see yourself as victim. And it allows you to commit altruistic evil, killing in the name of the God of life, hating in the name of the God of love, and practicing cruelty in the name of the God of compassion. It is a virus

that attacks the moral sense. Dehumanization destroys empathy and sympathy. It shuts down the emotions that prevent us from doing harm…. Victimhood deflects moral responsibility. It leads people to say: It wasn't our fault, it was theirs. Altruistic evil recruits good people to a bad cause. It turns ordinary human beings into murderers in the name of high ideas.[4]

This dehumanizing we/they thinking is what allows Jews to be scapegoated by other groups, and Rabbi Sacks sees this—and anti-Semitism in general—as a reflection of a greater breakdown of culture:

The scapegoat is the mechanism by which a society deflects violence away from itself by focusing it on an external victim. Hence, wherever you find obsessive, irrational, murderous anti-Semitism, there you will find a culture so internally split and fractured that if its members stopped killing Jews they would start killing one another. Dualism becomes lethal when a group of people, a nation or a faith, feel endangered by internal conflict.[5]

But it is our efforts to see ourselves in the face of the other that ultimately have the greatest power to heal the wounds of dualism and fuel the individual and collective work to combat divisiveness and hate. In these efforts the power of our core beliefs can change us and our enemies.

Rabbi Sacks cites the story of Csanad Szegedi, a member of the ultra-nationalist Hungarian political party Jobbik, which has been described as fascist, neo-Nazi, racist, and anti-Semitic. Szegedi was a rising young leader of the party until 2012, when he discovered he was a Jew and half his family had been murdered in the Holocaust. His grandparents were survivors of Auschwitz and were once Orthodox Jews but then decided to hide their identity.

Szegedi's understanding of the world changed completely in an instant. He resigned from the party, found a local Chabad rabbi with whom to study, became Shabbat observant, learned Hebrew, took on the name Dovid, and underwent circumcision.

Rabbi Sacks explains that "to be cured of potential violence towards the 'other,' I must be able to imagine myself as the other."[6] Before Szegedi's conversion he could not empathize with the other, the stranger. Now he had become the stranger, the despised Jew.

Learning to Love the Stranger

I believe that the most challenging commandment of all the 613 mitzvot in the Hebrew Bible is the one concerning our relationship with strangers: "The stranger who resides with you shall be to you as one of your citizens; you shall love him as yourself, for you were strangers in the land of Egypt: I Adonai am your God" (Leviticus 19:34). It calls for us to extend the personal love that characterizes relationships within a family or tribe into a broader form of love, a demand for justice for humanity as a whole. To love the stranger is to protect the stranger and to avoid at all costs being cruel or indifferent.

In 2005 the great rabbinic leader Rabbi Harold Schulweis (*z"l*) created Jewish World Watch, a unique nongovernmental organization made up of sixty American synagogues in Southern California that form an inter-congregational community. Its sole purpose is to fight genocide around the world, based on the principle that we are responsible as Jews for the well-being of everyone, and our responsibility requires us to do everything we can to fulfill the commandment, "You shall not stand idly by the blood of your fellow" (Leviticus 19:16, my translation).

In creating this organization, Rabbi Schulweis reminded the Jewish community that our duty to others extends not only from our Jewish religious tradition but also from our empathic identification with others who suffer. We know well the heart of the afflicted because we carry with us what our people suffered during the Holocaust.

David Suissa, president of the *Los Angeles Jewish Journal*, told me about a conversation he once had with Rabbi Schulweis in which David asked whether Jewish activism for non-Jewish causes diminishes our ability to care for our own people. The rabbi answered that the mitzvah to care for the stranger doesn't specify that we should care only about Jews. There's no either/or choice between caring for the stranger and caring for the well-being of Jews, he said. The Torah mentions the mitzvah to care for the stranger thirty-six times, and Rabbi Schulweis said that much of his great love for the Jewish people has to do with that emphasis on empathy and humanity.

A guiding verse from Leviticus directs us to "love your fellow as yourself" (Leviticus 19:18). But how can we love another whom we neither know nor understand? The verse itself offers the answer. We "love" that aspect of the stranger that's like us, created *b'tzelem Elohim*, in the divine image (see Genesis 1:27).

Each year I introduce this idea to the children I teach by sharing a story once told by the Baal Shem Tov (in Hebrew, "Master of the Good Name"; often shortened to "Besht"), the founder of modern Hasidism in Ukraine in the late seventeenth century.

One day the Besht summoned Sammael, the lord of demons, because the Besht wanted Sammael to perform some important task.

Sammael roared in rage at the Besht. "How dare you summon me up from my world! Up until now this has happened to me only three times: the hour when the Tree of Knowledge was violated, the hour when the Israelites created the golden calf, and the hour when Jerusalem was destroyed."

No one, however, could refuse the Besht, so powerful a soul was his— not even Sammael, who might be the equivalent of today's Star Wars' embodiment of evil, Darth Vader. So Sammael arrived a moment later in the Besht's yeshiva. Seeing him, the Master of the Good Name told his disciples to reveal their foreheads and turn to face Sammael. Inscribed on every forehead was the sign of the image in which God creates the human being—*b'tzelem Elohim*.

Upon seeing this holy stamp, the lord of the demons was deeply moved. Out of the bit of light apparently still in his heart, a bit that hadn't been eclipsed by the dark side, Sammael agreed to do exactly as the Besht had requested.

But before leaving on his mission, Sammael asked humbly, "O Sons of the living God, permit me to stay here just a little longer and gaze upon your foreheads."[7]

I love this Hasidic tale because it shows the nobility of the human soul. It suggests what the world might become if everyone, including those who are consumed by darkness and murderous fear of the other, were to look upon the face of every other human being and recognize that each of us is imbued with infinite value and worth, and that every human being bears the image of God (or life). We'd then understand that the destruction of any human being is a tragedy because it's the destruction not just of one person but of all future worlds that might come from that person. It's the destruction of the divine image in the world.

I tell this story to children and their parents each year when we read the first chapters of the book of Genesis. Every time I look into their eyes, I see sparks of recognition, light, wonder, appreciation, and understanding of our common human-divine essence and what's at stake when individuals fight and nations go to war.

I wish bridging the divide between peoples and religions were as simple as telling a story, but life is a bit more complicated than that. There's a natural tendency for like to stay with like, for us to gravitate to and associate only with people who are similar to us, who think like us, who are socioeconomically, culturally, ethnically, racially, religiously, tribally, and politically like us. Drawing close to the stranger often feels counterintuitive and dangerous.

My friend Rabbi Amy Eilberg has engaged for many years in facilitating interfaith and Jewish-Palestinian dialogue. She writes about slowly transforming the fear that separates us from the other:

> I begin my exploration of intergroup encounter with interreligious dialogue precisely in order to investigate this primal fear of difference and how it can be transformed into the joy of being enriched by acquaintance with "the other." This ability to transcend the instinct that associates difference with danger is one layer of the work of moving from fear to reflection and, perhaps, to acceptance, of allowing the "enemy" to become a friend.[8]

As a people, and as humans, we have been struggling to transcend this tribal instinct for eons. In the eighth-century Babylonian text *Avot d'Rabbi Natan*, the question is asked, "Who is the hero of heroes?"

The answer? "The one who makes an enemy into a friend" (23:1).

The Muslim tradition teaches the same truth: "Return evil with good and your enemy will become a devoted friend" (Qur'an 41:34).

Fear, however, puts us far too often in narrow straits, and that narrowness feeds on itself and alienates us from others (Psalm 118:5–6). The Hasidic tradition calls this narrowness of spirit *mochin d'katnut*, which I translate as "small or narrow mind," instead of *mochin d'gadlut*, "large or spacious mind."

When the Israelites left Egypt after years of enslavement, they were confined by small minds. It would take these former slaves forty years of wandering to give birth to a new generation whose thinking wasn't constricted by memories of enslavement and suffering. Instead, it was open and able to receive new ideas, regard the world as if with new eyes, hear God's, or Unity's, voice.

There's a famous story told about a Hasidic rebbe who overheard two men in a tavern talking. The first man asked his friend, "Do you love me?"

"Of course I love you."

"Do you know what hurts me?"

"I don't know."

The first man said, "How can you say you love me if you don't know what hurts me?"

This woeful ignorance of the other's heartache characterizes even some of our closest relationships. Why? Perhaps because we just haven't taken the time, for whatever reason, to listen closely enough to what's in the heart of the other. If this is true with our friends, it is much more so on a societal and international level.

In the stories and rituals of our religion, we are reminded to reach beyond ourselves to practice unity in small, practical ways so we can make it available to ourselves as we work for peace, justice, and love.

This is the wisdom embedded in our tradition, our teachings, our basic values. We discover so many approaches to our ancient and still thoroughly modern problems when we suspend disbelief in "religion" and look for the meaning inside ourselves, our tradition and teachings.

The struggle between our tribal and our universal human identities, between love and justice, between the in-group and the out-group, between us and them, is constant. The only way Jews and our world will survive, and all the peoples of the earth will thrive, is if all of us understand and respect not only who we are in our distinct tribal identities but also the inextricable link we have to each other in a shared fate and destiny.

We have to be able to talk to each other and come to know one another. Knowing each other will bring us greater understanding of each other and foster mutual respect. That's what we Jews mean by peace, *shalom.*

Love,
Dad

Part II

Love, Marriage, and the Jewish Home

Why I Support Couples Who Intermarry (and Agreed to Officiate at Their Weddings)

A Case Study in Listening to Your Own Voice

Dear Daniel and David:

Young people often ask me how they'll know if they're making the right decisions in their lives.

Initially—and I don't mean to be facetious by saying this—you'll know by how things turn out. We learn our preferences and what's right for us through experience, and in general I think it's good to try a lot of things before committing to a lasting course of action. From the time you were old enough to say "No!" you have each been making choices, working your way through decisions as small as "What's for lunch?" and progressing through whether to break up with someone, find a new job, or change your mind about what you believe. Each time, you learn a bit more about what feels good to you, what it's like to live with the consequences of a choice, and how your choices cumulatively determine the larger shape of your life.

Keep in mind that you'll make mistakes—sometimes more than once—and make decisions that are sensible for a while but then lose their luster and appeal. In those situations it's important to accept the change that's taken place, be gentle with yourself about your role in it, and cut your losses by disengaging from the situation—a job that wasn't what you wanted, a love relationship that worked better on a fantasy level than in reality, a friendship gone bad.

If your decision to disengage has an impact on other people, as I've always told you, be kind and honest. You don't have to say everything you think and feel, just enough to explain and leave. Don't attack or blame. Leave the situation with dignity and behave in such a way that if you see the person five or ten years from now, you'll be able to hold your head up, know that you left with your integrity intact, and have no regrets. At all times, be a mensch.

As you do this, you'll come to know yourself better and better. And when you approach the most significant decisions in your life—committing to a vocation and a partner, deciding how to express your identity as a Jew, marrying, deciding when and if to start a family—you'll have a more refined set of criteria, a more well-honed inner compass.

Yet I know it's possible to draw on all your experience, explore all your options, use all your discernment to be critical and self-critical about those options, and *still* wonder if you are making the right choice, especially when the stakes seem high. At such times, my best advice is to trust your intuition, your own inner voice, instead of thinking that a list of pros and cons will lead you to the best decision.

Listening to Your Own Voice

Twentieth-century philosopher Rabbi Joseph B. Soloveitchik captures the not-always-rational reality of our hearts and souls when he writes:

> The major decisions of [our lives] are made spontaneously and suddenly, in response to an aboriginal command from within, and are not necessarily dictated by external considerations or conditions, not necessarily affected by pragmatic considerations.... Decisions of faith, of marriage, choice of profession, solutions to financial problems ... and most pivotal resolutions in life are reached intuitively.[1]

As I think back, I see that virtually every major decision I've made in my life has come to me precisely in the way that Rabbi Soloveitchik describes. Though I harbored doubts and second-guessed myself, those initial intuitions turned out to be the truest reflection of who I am. It was intuition that led me to become a rabbi rather than a lawyer or an art historian; to marry your mother after falling in love at my first sight of her, even though that might have seemed risky after a failed first marriage; to start a family, though it might have seemed the time wasn't right; to take the position of senior rabbi at a then-struggling congregation called Temple Israel of Hollywood.

Not everyone in my life has been enthusiastic about my choices, my timing, the trade-offs they thought I'd have to make. Following my own intuition has often meant putting aside the priorities, values, opinions, and thoughts of others—family, friends, teachers, and mentors—many of whom are very wise, but aren't me. It has also meant distilling my own voice and my own sense of meaning from the many inspired voices of Jewish tradition. There are so many of them—the Hebrew prophets; rabbinic sages and mystics; Jewish and non-Jewish philosophers and poets; and contemporary Jewish leaders and thinkers in America, in Israel, and around the world. Given that Judaism is an ancient tradition with layer upon layer of wisdom and experience that enriches all that comes down to us, it's taken some sorting out to decide what's meaningful to me and what's not. That's something each of us does as liberal Jews, and it's one of the key factors that distinguishes liberal Judaism from traditional orthodoxy.

For Orthodox Judaism, "meaning" is one singular thing, strictly defined and found in following the law and in relationship to God and the covenant begun at Mount Sinai. But in liberal Judaism, we find meaning in deciding for ourselves the significance of the covenant between Israel and God. That doesn't mean rejecting tradition for the sake of modernity. Rather, it's a question of individual choice on the one hand and adhering to the standards that have been passed down to us by tradition on the other. As we choose one way or another, there is a necessary tension between our individual needs and the needs of the community. This inner tension ought to lead to an internal dialogue. The path forward is not easy to navigate, but it is fascinating and challenging, and ultimately it's deeply meaningful and Jewish.

We all hear a chorus of voices in our heads—voices of wisdom that help shape our values and principles, and voices that hold us back from following our hearts and fulfilling our dreams. We hear the voices of our mentors and teachers and wonder if we'll disappoint them by going our own way. We wonder what our communities will think and say about us if we take a less-traveled path. Then we sit with ourselves and ask which voices we still wish to hear and which we need to silence as we tune in to our own unique voice and seek its guidance.

That, I believe, was Rabbi Soloveitchik's greater teaching: that we need to be able to hear our own voice and allow it to speak to us and through us directly, rather than being filtered through the voices of others.

A Case Study: Shifting the Perspective of a Lifetime (and Embracing Intermarriage)

I know it can seem abstract, this talk about listening to your inner voice, so I'd like to show you how doing so led me to shift a strong, long-held belief and decide to officiate at weddings in which one partner isn't Jewish. This might be akin to deciding after years of study, encouragement, and training at a law firm to become a potter. The arguments, internal and external, for sticking to the original course seemed incontrovertible, like the law of gravity, until another perspective, a voice that was truer from the inside, demanded to be heard.

Four years ago had one of you told me you were in love with a woman who wasn't Jewish, I would have told you that it wouldn't be possible for me to officiate at your wedding. It's nothing personal, I might have explained. It has everything to do Jewish survival and continuity into and beyond your children's generation. Despite our small global population of between fourteen and seventeen million Jewish souls (depending on how you define "Jew") in a sea of more than seven billion, ours is the oldest continuous, surviving religious tradition anywhere in the world. We have walked the earth and put down roots everywhere on the planet since the days of Abraham and Sarah.

As we have developed our faith and tradition over those three and a half millennia, I would have explained, the wisdom of our sages has had much to offer the world. Our prophetic tradition expounds a vision of justice and mercy that has informed the development of international legal systems, a vision that is still sorely needed. Our rabbinic commitment to high ethical and moral standards has the potential to lift the quality of life everywhere. Our communal ethos of generosity and mutual responsibility is second to none among the peoples of the world. And our faith that every human being is created *b'tzelem Elohim*, in the divine image, is a principle that could bring greater peace, kindness, and justice into the world if all humanity behaved accordingly.

What does this have to do with whether I would perform your wedding ceremony? *Everything,* I would have said. If there is one existential threat to our people, it is the fact that today 70 percent of all marriages involving a Jew are intermarriages, while only fifty years ago the intermarriage rate was 10 percent. A recent Pew Study according to Dr. Steven M. Cohen's discussion of the results, has shown that 98 percent of children of inmarried Jewish couples tend to be raised Jewish, while only 25 percent of children of intermarried Jews are raised Jewish.[2]

Dr. Cohen determined as well that there's almost no chance at all that children will identify as Jews if they're raised in homes in which two religions are practiced or in which no religion is practiced. In such situations the most likely result is confusion, resentment, or alienation, or even worse, complete disinterest. There was also higher stress on the couple. Though many intermarried couples are stable and loving, the divorce rate in such unions is twice that of marriages in which both partners are Jewish.[3]

To me the numbers said, "You can't encourage marriages that will accelerate this drastic reduction in the number of children raised as Jews and lead to higher divorce rates. It's a matter of survival."

A thundering collection of other voices in my head supported that passionate stance. These voices from Judaic texts and tradition and from teachers and mentors taught me that I was ordained a rabbi to help fulfill three vital purposes: to preserve the integrity of the Jewish covenantal relationship with God, the viability of the Jewish family, and the survival and continuity of Judaism and the Jewish people. I'd lived with the certainty of those voices for decades, along with a voice that commanded, "Thou shalt not officiate at an intermarriage ceremony!"

When mixed couples approached me, I wished them well, but I could not in good conscience give them the blessing of joining them under the chuppah.

That was my official, unbending stance for thirty-three years.

And yet … even with statistics on my side, even with the raw facts of how precarious is our survival into the next generations, I was tortured each time I turned a couple away. I know love when I see it, and I've often seen it flourish between two people from different faith traditions. One can't help but honor and respect the love that flows between two people who wish to commit themselves one to another for the rest of their lives.

Members of our family, people I love, asked me to officiate at their interfaith weddings, as did dear friends. It became increasingly difficult to explain why I couldn't, because more and more of those couples wanted to maintain their connections to the synagogue and Jewish life—and they wanted to raise Jewish children.

I turned away members of our community—beautiful men and women I'd known from birth. I'd officiated at their parents' weddings, and when they were born I'd named them. I'd presided over their becoming bar and bat mitzvah. I was their tenth-grade teacher in preparing for Confirmation. I wrote them recommendations for middle school, high school, and college, and I vouched for them on their military and employment applications. I officiated at the funerals of their grandparents and, in some cases, their parents. But when they met their *beshert*, their intended one, I would not officiate at their weddings if their *beshert* was not a Jew.

"It's the principle of the thing," I'd tell myself. But my heart was torn and conflicted.

Then I began to notice a voice in my head that was pointing out a narrative, a persuasive counterpoint to the narrative that "intermarriage is our doom."

In most cases today, I realized, the two people who fall in love are indistinguishable from each other on most measures of values, interests, and background, except that one was raised Jewish and the other was raised in another faith tradition (most of whom are Christian, but there have been Muslims and Buddhists too). In most cases today, neither is particularly religious beyond the fact that Christmas and Easter are important to the Christian. Passover Seders, lighting the Hanukkah menorah, and attending High Holy Day services are important to the Jew.

When I met with couples and asked Jews what defines their Jewish identity, they talked about the importance of family, history, ethics, and tradition. When I asked Christians to define the role of religion in their lives, they spoke about the centrality of God and spirituality because they were raised to understand that religion is expressed in church through rite, ritual, and sacrament. They were legitimately confused that the person they loved did nothing particularly Jewish in everyday life but insisted that he or she had to be married by a rabbi and must raise the children as Jews.

"But you aren't religious?" the Christians would ask. And the Jews would respond, "What's God got to do with this?" The Christian partners were baffled, and the Jewish ones had no clue why. But if such couples wanted to understand each other, work toward their own definition of Judaism, and create Jewish homes, what benefit was there in standing in their way? They begged to do the hard work of understanding one another and claiming the tradition for themselves. Was it really better to say they were wrong or less than equal in our community for that?

My intuition told me no.

One Rosh Hashanah, after making my decision in my own heart, I invited every intermarried couple who belonged to our synagogue to attend services. I told them I wanted to offer them and their families a blessing of gratitude during worship that morning because they'd chosen to affiliate with our community and had made a commitment to raising their children as Jews.[4] At that time I estimated that there were three hundred such couples out of a total of nearly nine hundred family units (including couples without children, couples with children, single parents with children, and individuals; straight, gay, lesbian, and transgender) in our community. That meant that there were 150 Jews married to 150 people of other faith traditions, or no faith tradition, who actively participated in the life of our community.

At the service that morning, I told our congregation (you were there) that I'd come to the conclusion, based on the new reality in which we find ourselves, and the fact that many intermarried families were successfully raising their children as Jews at our synagogue, that I believed I could better serve the Jewish people by officiating at interfaith weddings. After thirty-three years it was time for me to change my policy.[5]

The congregation of more than eleven hundred people exploded in a sustained standing ovation.

We had always welcomed intermarried families in our congregation, but our warmth and love for them as individuals stopped short when I drew the line at marrying them. One non-Jewish man with whom I'm very friendly said it best after the close of the service: "John, I always felt welcome here. But now I feel like this synagogue is my home away from home."

After the cheering stopped, I explained there was a bit of "fine print" attached to my decision. Although all surveys indicate that intermarriage brings about a much lower rate of Jewish identification in succeeding generations, I said, I believe that the close personal relationships that are created and nurtured between intermarried couples and their rabbis, cantors, and synagogues can increase the likelihood that the couple and their children will identify as Jews. Though there are no statistics to confirm this, my instincts and my observation of our intermarried families and their children at Temple Israel tell me that it is true, and that can only be good for their Jewish identity and the viability of the Jewish community over the long term.

Today when a Jew and a non-Jew in our community come to me and tell me that both partners are willing to commit to a Jewish future, Jewish education for their children, and the creation of a Jewish home, I officiate happily at their chuppah—and that includes you, Daniel and David.

There's no guarantee, of course, that you and they will follow through on a promise to me, but making a promise to their rabbi—in your case, to your father—has to be enough. Truly, unless these couples raise their children as Jews, my decision may turn out to have been a huge mistake. But I don't believe it is. I believe that our whole community's appreciation of the importance of and commitment to Jewish continuity and survival underline the importance of including interfaith couples fully by letting them celebrate their marriages with our full blessing. What better way to invite them and their children into every aspect of our community's life?

I didn't, and don't, ask that non-Jewish partners convert. Conversion isn't appropriate for everyone and should never be undertaken to please the Jewish partner—or the parents or grandparents. My message to mixed couples, then and now, is this: Yes, come in. Judaism and this community want you to experience your sense of belonging here in a new and deeper way. We want to be able to love you, your spouse, and your children, and for you to be able to love us and give to us of your heart and soul as you desire. We want you to feel that you belong here, that when you are here you are home.

Rabbi Mordecai Kaplan, the founder of Reconstructionist Judaism in America, once spoke with my cousin Chuck Bay. Rabbi Kaplan asked him one day, while emphatically thrusting his finger into his chest, "Where do you belong?" Chuck told him the name of his Baltimore synagogue at the time, and Rabbi Kaplan said, "More important than what you believe is where you belong!"

This is an extraordinary statement from a man who was such a powerful intellect in twentieth-century American Judaism. He understood well that heart trumps belief, and that home is where the heart is.

As we welcome mixed couples fully into our community—as we welcome interfaith couples home—it becomes clear to me that intermarriage need not necessarily be a loss for the Jewish people or a tragedy for Judaism. Rather, it's an opportunity, a challenge, and in some cases, a precious gift.

That's the voice I've been hearing in my head the past few years—not the voice of my teachers and mentors who dissuaded me from officiating at intermarriages, but rather the voice that Rabbi Soloveitchik (though he would have cringed at my decision, as he was the embodiment of American Orthodox Judaism) describes as the "aboriginal command from within" that values the love between two people who have found their life mates and wish to consecrate their love.

Rabbi Soloveitchik writes that every human being is subject to two wills: a lower will, called *ratzon tachton*, and a higher will, called *ratzon elyon*. It's the higher will, he says, that distinguishes human beings from the rest of creation. The higher will is in the center of our spiritual identity and as such is our real identity. The higher will, he says, is "intuitive, dynamic, aggressive, and passionate. It bursts forth with fervor and emotional intensity. Its insights … are inspired with the breath of divinity…. [It gives birth to] decisions which are radical in nature, revolutionary, and decisive … [it] can change the direction of one's life."[6]

Listen carefully to yourself, to your own voice, to your higher will—even when you'll have to "disappoint" me or tune out other powerful voices in your head.

I trust you. Always trust yourself.

Love,
Dad

Love and Marriage

Dear Daniel and David:

The most important decision you'll ever make is who you marry. Work is important, as are your friendships, but everything pales in comparison to your choice of a spouse. I know this from both my life with your mother and my forty-plus years of experience counseling and marrying couples.

There's no simple, magical way to know if the person you love is the right mate for you, but there's a wealth of collective wisdom that can guide you. Over the years I have asked many couples who have been married a long time—thirty, forty, fifty, sixty, and once seventy years—what it was about their relationships that sustained them. Most answered in similar ways, with a dozen factors appearing again and again:

- Listen well to what's deepest in the other's heart.
- Be understanding and empathic.
- Laugh a lot and love sharing mundane everyday activities.
- Never take each other for granted.
- Say "I love you" often.
- Bring each other unexpected gifts at unexpected times.
- Accept each other's differences and stop trying to change the other.
- Be faithful and trustworthy.
- Keep each other's confidences.
- Feel loved and valued by the other.
- Don't harbor resentments, and avoid placing blame.
- Share much, but also have separate interests and passions.

Yet these generous commonalities and tendencies alone aren't enough to keep good-hearted people together. I know that every couple wants their marriage to work, but a high percentage of marriages fail. Why? That's the sixty-four-million-dollar question!

As Leo Tolstoy might put it, happy couples are all alike, but every unhappy couple is unhappy in its own way. Sometimes partners change and grow apart. Some people lose interest in each other and are no longer accepting of each other's differences. Others stop communicating and no longer share common concerns. Many become frustrated, disappointed, hurt by, and angry with each other. Religious and cultural differences, family friction, and financial stress may undermine trust.

But the major stressors in a marriage don't come out of nowhere. It's possible to spot the likeliest sources of tension long before rings are exchanged. When I perform marriage ceremonies, I meet with couples far in advance of the wedding so I won't be a stranger to them under the chuppah. I want to know them as a couple, understand their strengths and weaknesses, and explore with them what they love about each other—as well as explore where there's potential for difficulty down the road.

In our conversations we steer straight for the six hot-button topics in a marriage: power, sex, money, in-laws, expectations, and religion. Couples ignore their differences in these areas at their peril, and I encourage you to sit with your partner and talk about where you really stand. It's easy to assume that because you are crazy about someone you'll agree on issues such as whether saving money is important or whose family you'll stay with over the holidays. But you won't see eye to eye on everything. Talking through your differences before getting married will give you one of the best windows into how you'll navigate the most divisive issues of your marriage.

Power

Let's start with one of the explosives: conflict.

Do you and your partner fight and argue? If so, about what?

How long do your arguments last?

Do you go to sleep angry, or do you work through your differences before going to bed?

Do you fight fair? That is, when there's a disagreement, do either of you go for the jugular and demean the other or do you talk through differences without accusation and attack?

Do you know what your partner's hot-button issues are and what hurts him or her?

If you could, is there anything about the other that you would change? If so, what?

The last question on this squirm-inducing list is perhaps the most important, because the answer reveals the level of acceptance you have for your partner. Though human beings are able to change and adjust behaviors that annoy another person—we can all learn to put the cap back on the toothpaste, pick up our clothes, stop whistling, or get out of the habit of interrupting—essentially we are who we are, and we don't change fundamentally, at our core. The conflicts you have now, I tell couples, are likely to be the same conflicts you'll have decades from now. Your challenge is to manage those conflicts. Eliminate what's irritating or bothersome as best as you can, and then accept what you can't change.

Each person copes with conflict differently. We each also listen differently, and we need to be heard and acknowledged by our significant other in different ways. Your goal, when you feel you aren't getting what you need from the other person, ought to be to identify what you want and then communicate it without attacking, blaming, accusing, or being disagreeable. The only effective remedy when you feel slighted, diminished, ignored, or dismissed by your partner is honest talk and active listening, followed by acknowledgment of the other's feelings and mutual adjustment and accommodation.

As both of you work to do this, you'll find out where the power is in your relationship. In the best partnerships—the ones where power is shared—each person wants not only to reconcile after a fight or argument but also to defer to the other's needs. If that's not happening, and one or both of you can't find a way to bend or to come back together, you have a land mine on your path.

Sex

I know this is a question you may not particularly want to hear from your dad, but how's your sex life?

> Is your time in bed together fun, exciting, loving, and emotionally satisfying, or is it frustrating and unsatisfying?
>
> If something happens during sex that isn't good, what can you say and do to make it better?
>
> Is one of you overly demanding of the other, being selfish and self-centered, or is there mutuality and generosity?
>
> Are you both comfortable talking through the issues involved?

You may not want to be candid with me, but to have a lasting relationship you have to be open with each other. As with the question of power, the core issue in a strong sexual relationship is whether each of you is sensitive and responsive to the other's desires and needs. Sexual connection stretches far beyond the hoped-for physical, emotional, and spiritual chemistry and tactile pleasure that we enjoy when making love. It also includes trust, appreciation for the other, and the ability to communicate verbally and nonverbally.

Good sex is about good communication. Beyond the infatuation stage, communication is increasingly the most important part of lovemaking. This is even more true as we age. Despite the diminishment of the high testosterone and estrogen of young adulthood, couples continue to enjoy sexual intimacy well into their senior years and that emotional partnership is what's most sustaining over the long term.

Nurturing your connection will *keep* you connected, whatever form your lovemaking takes.

Money

Next tough question: How do you feel about money?

> Do you feel secure and empowered when you have savings, investments, property, and enough money to assure your financial security for the long-term?
>
> Do you tend to be a saver and spend conservatively?

Do you create budgets and stick to your plans, always with your long-term goals in mind?

Or:

Do you feel most empowered when you are able to spend freely?

Do you value that freedom over buying property, funding your children's educations, or planning for retirement?

Do you feel most happy and secure when you know that you are unrestrained and can do what you wish and buy what you want whenever you feel like it?

Parables about ants and grasshoppers aside, there is no right answer. The only imperative is that both of you be truthful about your deepest feelings. Money means different things to different people. Unless you understand what it means and symbolizes to each of you and arrive at consensus about how you'll manage your money, savings, spending, and planning, conflict is inevitable—and it may be fatal to your marriage. That's deeply sad, because conflicts about money can be avoided and managed like everything else—if expectations are out in the open and communication is clear.

Clarify with your partner where you each are on the continuum of saving and spending, and err on the side of oversharing. Don't think about getting married before you have agreed on financial goals and a financial plan and have found a way each of you can fulfill your needs. If you feel free and empowered when spending, for instance, you might set up a separate account to be used for that—until, of course, the funds are gone. If you need to have a nest egg to feel free, empowered, and secure, then you'll need a separate savings and investment plan so your needs will be met.

If you and your partner have similar attitudes toward money, especially if you are savers, you are fortunate. If you are both spenders, you'll definitely need a budget and financial plan. In all cases be sure to create an annual budget that includes everything—housing, children, education, food, entertainment, vacation, and luxury items. This budget ought to be as detailed as possible so you know exactly what you earn and what you spend. Include drinks you buy at the local coffee shop, what you spend at the cleaners, your clothing allowance, and haircut expenses. Most people are surprised by how much they actually spend when they detail it out.

I also encourage you to have concrete long-term financial goals that include housing, your children's college educations, and retirement. If you begin to plan and save in your twenties and contribute to retirement savings on a consistent basis, one day you'll actually be able to retire. I can't tell you how many people in my age group didn't adequately plan for retirement and can't retire when they want to—Social Security and a modest inheritance can't cover the style of living they want to maintain. I urge you to seek out and pay a qualified financial planner who will help you address your short-term and long-term needs.

Resentments and misunderstandings about money can turn toxic, so be sure to talk through these potentially contentious issues:

> If one of you enters the marriage with property, savings, a larger income, a trust fund, or family money, do you wish to share everything or do you want a prenuptial agreement?
>
> What are your hopes and expectations about sharing finances, if you share them?
>
> If you don't have much of an estate but your partner does and wants a prenup, how do you feel about that?
>
> Who decides what's spent and how?
>
> If you have equal net worth, how will you make decisions about saving and spending?
>
> Who will be the one to manage your finances?
>
> Who is smarter and better educated about money management between the two of you?
>
> Is your marriage an equal partnership or is it one in which each of you takes care of your own finances?
>
> Does one of you, consciously or unconsciously, regard money as a source of power relative to your partner?

Your answer to this last question—the most important one—will affect your answers to all the others, so consider it carefully and take your partner's perceptions as seriously as your own. If one of you realizes that money is a source of power to one person, you'll need to work out what money really means in your relationship. Equality and mutuality are the goals in a good marriage, no matter how much money each party has. A power imbalance here can quickly corrode your bond.

None of these questions can be put off. You'll have to discuss them openly, honestly, and in good faith. And if you find that you can't, note the red flags waving and consider talking to a trusted outside party—a parent, your rabbi, a counselor—about what's going on in the relationship.

In-laws

"What's the difference between in-laws and outlaws?" goes the old joke.

"Outlaws are wanted."

No matter how much you love your partner and his or her family, you probably won't be immune to the friction that's created when families come together. But identifying potential trouble spots can help you strategize around them. Ask yourself and each other:

> How do you get along with your own family?
>
> Where are the tensions in your family? Do they have the potential to create problems in your marriage?
>
> How do you relate to your partner's family?
>
> Are you equally family oriented?
>
> Do you share a similar need for family in your life?
>
> What are your extended family's expectations of you on Shabbat, Jewish holy days, Sunday brunch, Passover, High Holy Days, Labor Day, the Fourth of July, Memorial Day weekend, Thanksgiving, and New Year's?
>
> Will each partner's family be competing for your attention?
>
> How will you decide where to go, and how will you negotiate these demands with your families and with each other?

When I gather together the two sides of a family at the signing of the ketubah just before a wedding, I often say to the parents, "In this marriage, each side of the family is gaining a son or daughter and losing a son or daughter." On the one hand, there is now a larger family because of the joining together of this loving couple. But on the other hand, a new family is also being created and must be respected.

On the occasion of their children's marriage, parents must undergo an act of *tzimtzum*, contraction, to make space for the new couple to create a new family of their own; they must be given the privacy to do so. If you sense that this may not happen, make a plan for what you'll do and get help, if you need it, to set boundaries that will allow you to define for yourselves what your relationship to your larger tribe will be.

Expectations

What do you expect marriage to be like? What does a good husband do? A good wife? Each of you comes into your relationship with expectations of marriage based on what you experienced in your childhood homes with your own parent or parents. No two families are the same. While each of you may assume that you are talking about the same thing when you use the word *marriage*, your definitions may in fact be far apart.

But you can clarify your terms, your beliefs about your respective roles, and your expectations of the relationship by asking:

Were you raised in a two-parent family or a single-parent family?

Did one of your parents die young or abandon the family?

Did your parents divorce? If so, was there acrimony?

Did you grow up with a father and a mother, two mothers or two fathers, or a single parent?

Was there gender-role definition between your parents?

What gender definitions, if any, do you want or expect of yourself and from your partner?

Did your parents enjoy a happy marriage?

Did they show affection to each other in front of you?

Were they demonstrative or reserved in public?

Did they have fights in the home to which you were a witness?

What kind of emotional environment were you raised in?

Do you have a positive understanding of marriage or a skeptical one?

Be sure you have asked and answered all these questions and thought through their implications before you get married. I warn couples that when they walk away from the chuppah at their wedding and look at each other in those initial moments, it's as if an attic door has opened, releasing a flock of expectations about what it means to be a spouse to the other person. Even though you may know each other very well and love each other dearly, you are suddenly strangers dressed in new roles, entering a new realm of identity.

Those who understand how their feelings about marriage have been shaped by the parents who raised them—and are able to talk about that imprint with the other person—will necessarily navigate the waters of their young marriage with greater understanding and satisfaction.

All of this is true for both heterosexual and LGBTQ couples. Some issues are different, but marriages are similar, and the dynamics between people in committed love relationships are common across such differences. Many of your friends are LGBTQ, as are many members of our synagogue community. I don't make distinctions; nor should any of us.

Faith, God, Religion, and Culture

Finally, how will you meld your spiritual and cultural lives? How will you, as a couple, express your understanding of faith, God, Jewish tradition, religion, culture, and peoplehood?

You can take on this sweeping topic by asking:

Do you come from similar or different religious, cultural, national, and socio-economic backgrounds

How do you wish to raise your children?

If you should have boys, is there agreement on a Brit Milah?

How do you wish to create a Jewish home? (See my next letter for more on this.)

Remember this: there's twice as much divorce among partners who come from different religious and cultural backgrounds as there is in in-group marriages, in which both partners are Jewish.

That said, you'll love the person you love, and if you intermarry I hope you'll be among the many such couples who are happy and well-suited to each other. Our community is filled with mixed couples, and their relationships thrive because the partners work hard to bridge their differences with a great deal of discussion, active listening, empathy, mutual understanding, compromise, and sacrifice.

You have to be conscious of what will be expected of you by a partner of a different religious, cultural, or national background. Then you'll have to be prepared for whatever sacrifice you'll need to make for the sake of your spouse and your marriage.

Talk—and more important, listen—to bring all your invisible assumptions to the surface.

Nurture Each Other Well

Marriage is challenging always, and even the best marriages are good because the couples work very hard to make them that way. Nothing comes easy, but constant nurturing and close communication make for an enduring and ever-deepening marriage.

Your mother and I adore each other, and we're each other's best friends. We trust each other, rely on each other, and would do anything for each other and for you. Getting to this place has taken much effort, much love and patience, and a great deal of honest and frank communication. We have been married now for over three decades, and we have known each other for over one decade more. Without a doubt, finding your mom, falling in love with her, and deciding to marry her was the single most important and wonderful thing I've done in my life. Everything else has flowed from that—you boys, our life as a family, her work and mine, our friends and common commitments. No marriage is perfect, because no person is perfect. But your mom and I have been happy, and we have worked hard.

We're here as Jews to do many things, and one is to create in our homes a *mikdash m'at*, a small sanctuary, a place of intimacy and love, of faith and trust, of creativity and acceptance, of generosity, kindness, and joy. That's what our marriage has fed.

I've read the following poem at weddings over the years because it captures a depth of camaraderie and love that's uncommon but is present in the best marriages. I'm especially drawn to this poem because it reflects a depth of generosity, humility, gratitude, kindness, tenderheartedness, acceptance, and understanding of oneself in relationship to the other that could well be the standard toward which every one of us aspires with our beloved. Though many young couples attain such a relationship by the time they step beneath the chuppah, it often takes many years to realize and understand the poet's deeper sentiments.

This poem, often attributed to Roy Croft and based on a nineteenth-century German poem, is among my favorite wedding poems:

Love

I love you not only for what you are,
But for what I am when I am with you.
I love you not only for what you have made of yourself,
But for what you are making of me.
I love you for the part of me that you bring out;
I love you for putting your hand into my heaped-up heart
And passing over all the foolish, weak things
That you can't help dimly seeing there,
And for drawing out into the light
All the beautiful belongings
That no one else had looked quite far enough to find.
I love you because you are helping me to make of the lumber of my life
Not a tavern but a temple,
Out of the works of my every day
Not a reproach but a song.
I love you because you have done more than any creed could have done
To make me good, and more than any fate could have done to make me
     happy.
You have done it without a touch, without a word, without a sign.
You have done it by being yourself.
Perhaps that is what being a friend means, after all.

My hope for you is that you will each discover a deeply satisfying and sustaining love with the one you cherish.

     Love,
     Dad

Creating a Jewish Home

Dear Daniel and David:

As I imagine each of you creating a meaningful, loving Jewish home with your life partner someday, I want to share a story that warms the heart and opens the soul, for it's on the level of heart and soul that two people lay the foundation for a life together.

The legend goes that when the angels heard that God was about to create the divine image and emanate it into the world, they conspired to hide it. One angel proposed putting God's image on the top of a mountain. A second suggested hiding it at the bottom of the sea. But the wiliest angel of all said, "Let's hide it by putting it in each man and woman, because that's the last place anyone will look for it."

Some say that the soul, the *neshamah*, is God's breath, based on the meaning of the word's Hebrew root, meaning "to breathe." Others say the soul is pure light, and all earthly light is only a faint glimmer of this divine radiance. Whatever its nature, it's hidden within us. But as we recognize this light first in a lover's eyes, then in our children, our families, and the people we love, we can reflect it back and so illuminate our homes and communities with the light of the soul.

Perhaps you remember God's words to Moses: *Asu li mikdash v'shachanti b'tocham*, "Make for me a sanctuary that I may dwell within them" (Exodus 25:8, my translation). Each of us, and each home we create, is potentially a *mikdash m'at*, a small sanctuary, wherein the mundane becomes the holy, and the holy opens our hearts to be able to love more freely and deeply. The love you share, the way you welcome guests, the kindness you show each other, the ethics you practice—all these sanctify your home as a place wherein dwells the very best of who you are and the very best of who *we* are as Jews.

I know how challenging it can be day in and day out to try to elevate love and to remember how sacred our connection to each other is. Life's annoyances and pressures mount, and poetry retreats. The holy feels mundane. So I'd like to recommend the best means I know for replenishing and inspiring yourself as you each build a life and home with your partner: observing Shabbat.

Shabbat takes us back to the first light, to the mythic and mystic Garden of Eden, and effects a reunion with our innermost selves, with our souls, our loved ones, our people, and God. Shabbat is a rekindler of divine light, a restorer of soul, a bridge linking heaven and earth. It's also, not insignificantly, the time when Jews come together to sing. I add my voice to a growing chorus when I say that Shabbat is our tradition's greatest treasure, its best kept secret, and a natural antidote for what's missing in our busy daily routines.

By observing Shabbat you create a bit of paradise each week in your home and in the synagogue. Rabbi Nachman of Breslov says that "the most direct way to attach ourselves to God in this material world is through music and song. Even if you can't sing well," he says, "sing. Sing to yourself. Sing in the privacy of your home. But sing."[1]

Nobel laureate and Holocaust survivor Elie Wiesel (*z"l*), in his book *The Jews of Silence*, tells of traveling to the former Soviet Union in the late fifties to see if there were any Jews left. He stood outside the great synagogue in Moscow on Simchat Torah and witnessed thousands of people singing. He couldn't believe what he heard. He approached a young woman in her twenties and asked her, "Are you Jewish?" She nodded.

"What do you know about being Jewish?"

She answered, "I don't know anything. But my grandfather told me that Jewish people sing."[2]

We Jews have always sung. Miriam led the people singing and dancing with timbrels on the edge of the sea. King David, the poet of the Psalms, is called the "sweet singer of Israel" (2 Samuel 23:1). Torah is chanted. The Talmud is chanted. The Haggadah is chanted. In Eastern Europe Jews traveled long distances to hear a hazan's sweet and soulful voice. Black

Baptists, God bless them, didn't invent soulful singing. We Jews have been doing it for centuries.

I'm convinced that through song God's light glows as if on the first day of creation. The light hidden in the human soul is brightened through song. Rabbi Abraham Joshua Heschel teaches: "There are three ways in which a man expresses his deep sorrow: the man on the lowest level cries; the man on the second level is silent; the man on the highest level knows how to turn his sorrow into song. True prayer is song."[3] Singing brings us closer to the place where no words need to be uttered and no sound needs to be heard. Poetry lifts the spirit and evokes wonder. Song and silence join us with our *neshamot*, our godly souls.

Through song, I believe, our separate lights can stream together and create a single blaze. But we need to sing and be part of a singing community, one voice sustaining another, one soul linked to a thousand kindred spirits, many souls united in one voice, in one joyful calling out.

Think back to when you were very little and you sang everything. Small children do this naturally and constantly. When we grow up, we muffle the song in ourselves, and for some of us, it dies. But our souls still want and need to sing.

And then they want to rest.

That aspect of Shabbat, its directive to unplug from the world of work and commerce, seems particularly welcome these days, when so many of us find that our lives are overprogrammed, disjointed, and filled with stress. Jews across the country are concluding that living in the fast lane all the time isn't everything it's cracked up to be and that our tradition provides the antidote we really need: a day simply to be without doing, a time to love without feeling lonely, an opportunity to celebrate without worrying, a moment to retrieve simplicity and dispel clutter.

This radical and ancient notion, one that the Jewish people gave as a gift to the world more than three thousand years ago, offers us a way to rediscover our families and friends. It also offers the inherent wisdom of our taking one day to exist in the world without having to change or transform it. Twentieth-century philosopher and theologian Rabbi Milton Steinberg notes that the secret to good living is to cultivate the dual ability to passionately embrace life and then let it go.[4] Nothing gives a person the practice of letting go as does Shabbat. Shabbat can encourage us to persevere through frantic or stressful days as we look forward to the promise of rest and restoration at the end of the week. Los Angeles–based spiritual leader Rabbi Naomi Levy writes,

> The days preceding the day of rest become days of excitement and expectation. Even the most harried workdays become tolerable when you know a day of holy peace is shortly arriving. The days succeeding the day of rest become days of light too. They shimmer with the after-glow of a revived spirit. True rest gives us a completely different per-spective on all of our difficulties. It allows us to heal, to reflect, to give thanks, and to face whatever lies ahead with a renewed sense of calm.[5]

I know how hard you work, how much you love the release of going out on the weekend, but I hope you'll each consider creating a Shabbat tradi-tion at home, and perhaps at the synagogue as well, and give yourself the gift of Shabbat every week—or as often as you can. The replenishing rest of Shabbat spills over into our weeks, our years, our lives—and it's good for more than the soul. There's evidence from a study conducted at Duke University that those who attend religious services once a week and are part of a caring religious community add years to their lives, reduce stress, and end up in the hospital significantly less than those who don't pray in community.[6]

My week would be intolerable without Shabbat in one form or another. When you lived at home, the four of us sang the blessings together over lights, wine, and challah. Then we ate a good meal, during which we talked, laughed, and shared whatever was going on in our lives. Doing this together centered all of us. You'll recall our family tradition of holding hands when we sang the candle blessing. We offered each other blessings, and though you protested when you were little, I made use of my prerogative as your dad to invoke upon you the traditional blessing of parents on their children and the *birkat kohanim* (the priestly blessing). It was important for me, as your father, to do this. And when and if you are graced with children of your own, I hope you'll invoke upon them the very same blessing that Jewish parents have said *l'dor vador*, from genera-tion to generation, for more than three thousand years.

I hope that even now you each will consider ways to make your home *kosher*, uniquely Jewish. This includes not only what you put into your mouth but also what comes out of your mouth. I hope you each consider linking yourself in the *sharsheret hakabalah*, the chain of Jewish history, tradition, and peoplehood, by filling your home with fine Judaica and Jewish art, building a substantial Jewish library, and putting a mezuzah on your doorpost. Create a beautiful sanctuary for yourself and your partner, for your family, for your soul. Establish a joyful place where Shabbat and holidays are celebrated, song is heard, and ideas are shared and debated; where you engage in conversation about ethics, politics, culture, the arts, and Jewish life—a place where Torah abides.

I know each of you will do this in your own way. As you do, I have faith that you will each create a home with your spouse and children that is worthy of respect and filled with meaning and joy. I look forward to being a part of your life there.

Love,
Dad

Part III

Living in the World of Good and Evil, War and Peace

Embracing Shades of Gray and Finding
Peace in the World and at Home

Dear Daniel and David:

What I want for you, for me, and for the world is peace. Pursuing it is my mission as a rabbi and teacher. It's so important to me that I sign all my emails and head my blog with this statement from *Pirkei Avot*, the Sayings of the Sages: "Be a disciple of Aaron—loving peace and pursuing it; loving people and bringing them to Torah" (1:12).

This Mishnah text advocates that every Jew (and I believe it should be every human being, regardless of tradition) ought to be a *rodef shalom*, a pursuer of peace. Another text reminds us that *pursuing* peace takes action and commitment, not mere wishing: "If a person sits in his place and is silent, how can he pursue peace among people, between each and every one? Rather, one should go out from one's own place and go searching in the world and pursue peace among people" (*Avot d'Rabbi Natan* 12).

Great, we all say. Let's do it!

But how? For all our desire, we seem to be terrible at achieving peace. I know no one who doesn't claim to want it. People desire peace for themselves, their families, friends, communities, and nations. Even those who wage war say they fight for the sake of peace. Yet we fail miserably and consistently at attaining it.

Part of the problem is that most of us aren't clear about what peace is. I think we can transform our understanding by taking a new tack and asking not "What is peace?" but rather "What's the opposite of peace?" When I frame the question that way, most people say the opposite of peace is war, and that's true. A more revealing answer, though, is that the opposite of peace is Truth, with a capital *T*.

Truth is a commonly discussed value in philosophy and religion. Its nature is abstract, theoretical, and conceptual, pointing to an ideal and absolute state that doesn't exist in real life. Capital-*T* Truth requires an unbending, no-nonsense approach to life and relationships. Truth creates dichotomies: either/or, black/white, right/wrong, good/evil. It's exact and exacting, uncompromising, precise, rigid, and hard. There are no gray areas in Truth.

By contrast, peace is expansive and open, embracing and inclusive. It's soft, down-to-earth, and complex. Peace results not from various parties pursuing their separate Truths but rather from accommodation, cooperation, concession, conciliation, and compromise. Peace needs shades of gray. It's nuanced and never cut-and-dried.

Peace isn't a zero-sum game in which one side's Truth eclipses the other's. For a peaceful, stable, and sustainable resolution of conflict over the long term—whether in international or national arenas; between ethnic, tribal, or religious groups; in the workplace; between friends; in marriages; or within families—each side must be seen, heard, understood, and respected. Each side needs to be able to claim at least a limited victory and to emerge with its dignity and self-respect preserved.

Peace must be win-win; any agreement that comes without each side feeling that it has attained some of its goals won't stand. Peaceful compromise prevents either side from later asserting that it landed a knockout punch and was completely victorious. In any successful negotiation, each side must come away a little happy and a little unhappy.

Recall Egyptian president Anwar Sadat's journey to Israel in 1977, which resulted in the Camp David Accords. Egypt had been humiliated by Israel's lightning victory in the 1967 Six-Day War, in which Israel destroyed the entire Egyptian air force while it still sat on the ground.

Before President Sadat could ever make peace with Israel, he knew that he had to restore his nation's dignity and honor, so he launched the 1973 Yom Kippur War on the Jewish people's holiest day and caught Israel unaware. Though Israel would eventually soundly defeat his country on the battlefield, Sadat was able to claim at least a limited victory because of Egypt's initial surprise onslaught against Israeli troops on Sinai's Bar Lev Line.

That helped Egypt regain its national pride and allowed Sadat, through his peace deal, to offer what Israel had yearned for since the establishment of the State but had never received: acceptance as a sovereign nation by its largest Arab neighbor. In exchange Israel gave up for the sake of peace the entire Sinai Peninsula, including its oil wells and airfields.

Shalom: A Peace That Flows from Equality

Religious and nationalist ideologues and extremists—and members of our families who are alienated and at war with each other—will never attain peace and reconciliation with their adversaries as long as they insist upon their Truth being preserved in its totality. Peace requires that the parties take their two irreconcilable Truths and choose: if they want Truth, they should get ready for war; if they want peace, they must surrender, at least in part, Truth.

Jewish tradition recognizes that while both peace and Truth are high virtues, they can't coexist in human settings. If we want peace, we must choose its softness over the hard inflexibility of Truth, giving up our unforgiving Truths for the malleability of peace. Truth is exclusive; peace is inclusive. Truth is absolute; peace embraces difference.

It's not surprising that the second-century CE Palestinian sage Rabbi Yehoshua ben Korha stated that before rendering an opinion in a court of law, judges must first suggest to litigants that they compromise and come to a peaceful resolution of their dispute. Compromise leading to peace is so important a value in Judaism that the Talmud considers it a mitzvah (*Avot d'Rabbi Natan* 12).

The Jewish concept of peace differs dramatically from its Roman counterpart *pax* (Latin for "peace"). In the Roman republic one was either slave or free. As long as the peace was kept—that is, this social order was sustained and stable—all was well. Justice wasn't a factor.

But in Judaism a state of *shalom* (peace) presumes that every human being is equal by virtue of having been created *b'tzelem Elohim*, in the divine image. Any human act that diminishes another human being is in effect diminishing God and reflects an absence of *shalom*.

Shalom points to an overarching state of harmony and balance that's far greater than the sum of its parts. It's a condition "of well-being, tranquility, prosperity, and security, circumstances unblemished by any sort of defect." *Shalom* "is a blessing, a manifestation of divine grace [*chesed*]." [1]

The theme of peace has a dominant presence in Jewish tradition—the word *shalom* appears 314 times in the Hebrew Bible; 1,890 times in the Talmud; 784 times in the *Midrash Rabbah*; and 332 times in the *Zohar*.[2] So highly is *shalom* regarded in Jewish tradition that all the benedictions and prayers of the Jewish liturgy conclude with an invocation for peace.

We usually think of peace in the context of relations between and among nations. However, it's important to note that most of those 3,320 passages in Jewish literature on peace aren't concerned with macro issues. They refer instead to our relationships with each other, within our families, and with people of other faith traditions and national identities.

A category of law developed in the Talmud is based on the principle of *mipnei darchei shalom*, things we do "for the sake of the ways of peace." For example, the Talmud says, "Our rabbis taught: 'We support the non-Jewish poor along with the poor of Israel, and visit the non-Jewish sick along with the sick of Israel, and bury the non-Jewish poor with the dead of Israel, for the sake of peace [*mipnei darchei shalom*]" (*Gittin* 61a). *Mipnei darchei shalom* embraces our practical concerns about how we get along with each other and our neighbors as well as the virtue of altruism.

I recall a conversation I heard between Rabbi Alexander Schindler (*z"l*), then president of the Union of American Hebrew Congregations (now the Union for Reform Judaism), and a large group of delegates to the Reform movement's biennial convention. In an open discussion one woman asked him, "Rabbi, there are so many important Jewish and non-Jewish causes to which we can contribute our *tzedakah* [charitable giving]. As a Jew I want to support my people. My question is, given that the Jewish people's needs are so great and endless, do I give to non-Jewish causes as well?"

Rabbi Schindler answered, "You have to contribute to Israel and our Jewish causes because if not us, then who? But you have to contribute to everything else as well, not only because it's the morally responsible thing for Jews to do and it nurtures our altruistic impulses, but also *mipnei darchei shalom*, for the sake of the ways of peace between us and the world."

We contribute to the victims of disasters when they occur around the world, not just as Americans or as Israelis (Israel, reflecting fundamental Jewish values and an understanding of enlightened self-interest, is often the first respondent to such tragedies) but as Jews, in an altruistic spirit and *mipnei darchei shalom*, for the sake of the ways of peace. The same applies to local causes that help the homeless, the poor and food insecure, those without jobs or health care, those who are disabled and in need of public support, battered women and children.

This larger understanding of peace motivates Reform Jewish advocacy in America, through our movement's social justice commission and the Religious Action Center of Reform Judaism in Washington, DC. We work to raise the minimum wage to a livable level and to support economic justice. We advocate on behalf of universal health care and push for reasonable gun safety laws and racial justice. We support women's and LGBTQ causes, and efforts to protect the environment and encourage sustainable living. We press for medical research to find treatments for a host of diseases, rare and common. Peace also drives our work on a wide range of other causes that support and enhance the dignity of every human being. We see it as part of our Jewish mission in this country to act on behalf of others here and throughout the world.

Peace in the Family

As challenging as all the world's big issues are, they sometimes seem less daunting than the ones we face as we try to bring the qualities of peace into our homes. One of the saddest and most frustrating aspects of my life as a congregational rabbi has been that I'm continually witness to a powerful absence of peace within families and in every social setting. Many people wound each other, give and endure harsh and hurtful speech, and harbor petty jealousies and misunderstandings. Many are hurt, angry, resentful, and alienated from each other.

Sometimes these wounds and hurts destroy relationships, and healing is necessary for the individuals involved to move forward. Sometimes with attention and help, damaged relationships can be salvaged. But many of us give up; we're afraid to confront those who have wronged us, assuming that the other is so wedded to his or her Truth and we're so wedded to ours that no one will budge or make accommodations. We stubbornly and foolishly back ourselves into corners, take strong and absolute stands, and become resigned to our situations as they are. We're reluctant to expose ourselves to more pain and hurt, and too proud to revisit the relationships and make changes, especially after a long time has passed.

We might be right—there may be little or no hope for reconciliation with the offending or offended other. But we might be wrong too. Meeting the other person, reaching out, might initiate a process of *t'shuvah* (return), *s'lichah* (forgiveness), and *achdut* (unity or reconciliation). When a situation is particularly difficult, the presence of a mediator, therapist, or rabbi can make a conversation easier.

I encourage you to follow any impulses you have toward reconciling with those from whom you feel estranged. Attaining peace is among the highest Jewish aspirations because only through relationship can we be restored to each other, and ultimately to ourselves, and affirm the Unity principle at the core of Jewish tradition.

I know there are occasions when peace is impossible because one or both parties are so rigid and uncompromising that little can be accomplished. In those cases I advise that contact be limited as much as is humanly and realistically possible. In the case of a marriage or partnership, this likely means divorce or separation.

But don't dismiss the possibility that peace will win over Truth in a damaged relationship.

One High Holy Day season years ago, I spoke about the theme of forgiveness in one of my sermons, a classic subject during the Days of Awe. That day a certain woman and her mother-in-law came to services. The two women's relationship had gotten off on the wrong foot, and then they continued to offend each other for the next twenty years. Finally they had silently decided to ignore one another as much as possible. But the tension between them remained, and there was no real peace in the family.

In my sermon I called upon people to let go of old grievances that kept them imprisoned in jails of their own making. A week later I received a letter from the mother in-law, who told me that she and her daughter-in-law went home after the service, looked at each other, and decided that nothing was so important that it should keep them from getting along much better. Now, she wrote, they were determined to do so. It was a turning point for them both, and all it took was swallowing their pride, acknowledging that the other had a legitimate story and a legitimate Truth, and that each of them had to set aside her own story and Truth for the sake of their family and future.

At this point in my life, I know who my friends are, and there's nothing I will deliberately do to offend anyone I deeply care about. It just isn't worth it. Life is way too short to sacrifice friendship for Truth. One of my cousins told your mom and me recently that she will never say anything that will offend her friends. They are too important to her, she said. As a result she has friends going back to her childhood whom she adores and who adore her.

You guys are still young, and the only advice I can offer you as you navigate your personal lives and search for your own peace is to strive always to keep your friends close. Treat them with respect and dignity. Be kind at all times and do whatever it takes—without losing your integrity and dignity—to maintain these relationships. The friendships we make when we're young become increasingly important as we get older. Trust me on this one. Choose peace always over Truth.

Love,
Dad

Why Your Generation Should Care about Israel's Future

Dear Daniel and David:

Israel is far away, a tiny country no larger than the state of New Jersey, with only 7.5 million people. Yet it's always in the news. Tragically, Israel lives in a bad neighborhood, surrounded by terror, violence, instability, and war. Arab rejectionists still deny Israel's legitimacy as the nation-state of the Jewish people and they want to destroy it. And in the territories across the Green Line—that is, the armistice line established in 1949 by a separation of forces between Jordan and Israel after the War of Independence—Palestinians have lived for nearly fifty years under Israeli occupation, without democracy and ruled by the Israeli military administration. Despite efforts to find peace in a two-states-for-two-peoples final resolution of the conflict, negotiations on several occasions have failed to produce an agreement that satisfies both Israel's security needs and Palestinian national rights.

The tragedy is that two peoples claim the same land as their own; both have been unwilling to compromise for the sake of peace; and hearts on both sides have hardened.

It's easy for many American Jews to get disgusted and angry, to feel alienated from the State of Israel and turn away in exasperation. Though I know you love Israel as I do, many of your Jewish friends don't understand what the modern State of Israel is or the complexities in the Israeli-Palestinian conflict. Or they hold Israel to unrealistic standards, and then when it inevitably fails to meet those standards they turn away.

I hope this letter will reinforce your resolve to stand by the democratic Jewish State of Israel. I also hope you will persuade those among your millennial friends and others who may not know enough—or who are distressed by the lack of a resolution of the Israeli-Palestinian conflict—to learn more, visit Israel often, and stay connected.

Though polls indicate that the majority of American Jews still support Israel, it's a tragedy of immense proportions for the Jewish people that far too many American Jews have washed their hands of Zionism and turned their backs on the State of Israel. Israel is crucially important to all of us. Its fate ought to be of ongoing central concern to you, your peers, and the entire American Jewish community.

We have discussed Zionism and the State of Israel throughout your lives. You know how I think as a liberal Zionist. Forgive my repetition, but I want to identify myself as a Zionist to make clear my perspective.

I'm a Jewish nationalist on the liberal left of the political spectrum. I believe that the establishment of the State of Israel is the greatest accomplishment in modern Jewish history and that it's incumbent upon Jews everywhere to do everything to assure its survival and viability as a liberal democracy and as the national home of the Jewish people.

By any metrics Israel is one of the world's great nations and democracies. It isn't perfect; no democracy is. Israelis' accomplishments there since 1948 and even before—going back another fifty years—are without parallel anywhere in the world. But none of what Israel has come to be is a given in the future. Even though Israel is the most powerful nation in the Middle East, there are legitimate threats to the Jewish state from the outside, and there are serious threats from within.

Soon after the 1967 war, David Ben-Gurion, the father of the Jewish state, Israel's first prime minister and minister of defense, came out of retirement from his kibbutz at Sde Boker in the Negev to make a prescient public statement. Israel, he said, was confronted with an historic and fateful choice. When it had been confronted by the combined armies of Egypt, Jordan, Syria, and Lebanon before June 5, 1967, it faced a war of extinction. But Israel was victorious in that war that lasted only six days. When the fighting stopped, Israel had conquered a vast territory, including the Golan Heights, the Sinai Peninsula, the West Bank, East Jerusalem, and the Old City. Fatefully, its decisions about how to govern that territory would shape its future.

From 1948 to 1967 Israel's majority had been Jewish, and its form of government was a parliamentary democracy. In Israel's Declaration of Independence, all Israeli citizens were guaranteed equal rights, regardless of their religion, gender, or race. This included Arab citizens of Israel.

Ben-Gurion said that Israel could retain and annex all the land it had conquered in the 1967 war and give equal citizenship, including the right to vote, to all its residents and thereby remain democratic, but it risked losing its Jewish majority. Alternatively, it could rule over the Arab population of three million in the occupied territories formerly in Egypt, Syria, and Jordan, but not grant equal rights or the right to vote to those residents, and cease being a democracy while retaining a Jewish voting and citizenship majority.

To this day Israel remains a democracy for Israeli citizens living within the Green Line, including the half million Jewish residents living in settlements around Jerusalem and in the West Bank. However, Israel isn't a democracy for the noncitizen Arabs living in East Jerusalem and the West Bank. Those Arabs have been ruled for nearly fifty years by an Israeli military administration and judged by Israeli military courts.

Your Frustration Makes Perfect Sense—*Use* It

In October 2014 I received an email from Sarah, a rabbinical student who grew up in our congregation and whose parents and extended family are lifelong Zionists. She was living in Jerusalem and had become disheartened by events and trends she observed in the State of Israel.

Sarah rightly perceived a growing corruption of classic liberal Zionist principles. She was shocked by growing racism in Israeli society, dismayed by the way the Israeli government envisioned the situation with the Palestinians, and befuddled by ongoing Jewish settlement building in the West Bank and home demolition in East Jerusalem. It horrified her that a liberal democracy could tell Israeli Arab citizens that they could no longer work in Israeli Jewish communities because they posed a "security threat."

Sarah wrote me that she feared that demagogic and oppressive forces were gaining popularity in Israel and that the Israeli government was becoming increasingly intransigent and ineffective in dealing with its many challenges.

She was disheartened as well that the chief rabbinate maintained coercive control over much of religious life in the state, and she wondered whether it would be preferable to give up Israel's Jewish character for the sake of preserving Israel's progressive democracy.

It was hard for her to feel any love for Israel, she said, and she confided that she felt like a heretic. She didn't know what to do or how to think about the Jewish state going forward.

In response I wrote an open letter not only to her but to all American Jewish liberal young people who were feeling this disconnection with the State of Israel. This is part of what I said:

Dear Sarah:

First, I want you to know that I'm proud of you, of your critical thinking, of your commitment to live an enriched Jewish religious and ethical life, to be a learned Jew, and of your yearning to make sense of what Israel means to you.

Second, you aren't alone. Shabtai Shavit, former director general of Mossad (Israel's security service), recently wrote about his similar concerns about the "future of the Zionist project" and the threats against it in the region and international community. Shavit harshly criticized Israel's political leadership's "haughtiness and arrogance, together with more than a bit of the messianic thinking that rushes to turn the [Israeli-Palestinian] conflict into a holy war."

Shavit worried that "large segments of the nation … have forgotten … the original vision of Zionism: to establish a Jewish and democratic state for the Jewish people in the Land of Israel" and that "the current defiant policy" of settlement building "is working against" this vision.

He called upon Israel to enter into conversation with moderate Arab nations (i.e., Jordan, Egypt, and Saudi Arabia) and negotiate, based on the Arab Peace Initiative of 2002, a two-states-for-two-peoples resolution of the Israeli-Palestinian conflict that would augur, as promised in the plan, the complete normalization of relations between Israel and the moderate Arab and Muslim world.

Shavit concluded soberly: "I wrote the above statements because I feel that I owe them to my parents, who devoted their lives to the fulfillment of Zionism; to my children; to my grandchildren; and to the nation of Israel, which I served for decades."[1]

As a rabbi who has served American congregants for thirty-six years and been an active Reform Zionist all that time, I offer ten additional thoughts to you and the young liberal American Jewish community, as well as others, if this applies:

1. You aren't alone in your worry about the dangers to the Zionist dream.
2. You aren't alone in your concerns about the unequal treatment of Arab citizens of Israel.
3. You aren't alone in your anger about the hegemony of the chief rabbinate over the lives of all Israelis.
4. Israel is far more than Jerusalem, which is becoming increasingly more ultra-Orthodox and right-wing. It's also Tel Aviv, a society that represents a modern Israel that can inspire you anew about Israel's past, present, and future.
5. Israel isn't a "racist society," though there are Israeli racists, a distinction with a difference.
6. Remember to appreciate that Israel remains a vital democracy despite its flaws and its current (but resolvable) status as an occupying force in the West Bank.
7. Don't be cavalier about Israel's real security threats, but don't accept at face value that those threats necessarily legitimate every policy executed by this government as smart, just, democratic, and moral.
8. Don't forget that many Israeli liberal human rights organizations monitor and fight injustice in Israel, East Jerusalem, and the West Bank.
9. You must be able to hold at the same time your conflicting thoughts and feelings about Israel while maintaining your active engagement with it.
10. Despite your disappointment, anger, and frustration, we can't afford for you to disengage from Israel. Though we aren't Israelis, and only Israelis can make the decisions vital to their lives

and security, we liberal lovers of Israel need you to become
our next generation's leaders in American Zionist organizations
that advocate for the democratic, pluralistic, nation-state of the
entire Jewish people.

We need you to keep the faith and become the advocates that Israel
deserves and that we and the Jewish people need.

Much love,
John

To that letter, I want to add a few thoughts.

The Promise of Israel Is More Than Theoretical

Though Zionism is a relatively new phenomenon in Jewish history—it's
only about 130 years old—I believe that to be fully Jewish today means
being a Zionist in the most basic sense: we Jews are tied to the destiny
and fate of the State of Israel no matter where we live. Israel's existence,
values, and policies have a direct impact upon our values and standing in
the world. Israel's strength and security affect our strength and security.

Israel presents the greatest moral and ethical challenge to the Jewish
people in two millennia. For the first time we have the opportunity to
live as a people with sovereign power to maintain and evolve our ethical
tradition.

Being Jewish means above all accepting that opportunity and responsibility. It's not enough to simply feel Jewish in our kishkes. It's not enough
to nurture Jewish families and raise Jewish children. It's not enough to
support our synagogues and promote Jewish education and culture. It's
not even enough to support the State of Israel in all the ways that are possible today.

The prophet Isaiah, speaking for God, said "I, Adonai, have summoned you [*ani Adonai k'raticha v'tzedek*] and I have grasped your hand.
I created you, and appointed you a covenant people" (Isaiah 42:6, my
translation). "It is too little that you should be My servant in that I raise up
the tribes of Jacob and restore the survivors of Israel: I will also make you
a light of nations [*or la-goyim*] that My salvation may reach the end of the
earth" (Isaiah 49:6).

These Isaiah passages promise the ancient Israelites that God would restore them to their land and cause other nations to open their eyes and look to the people of Israel as a symbol of just, compassionate, and peaceful living.

The prophet called upon Israel to be a *rodef shalom*, a pursuer of peace, to

> Beat their swords into plowshares
> And their spears into pruning hooks:
> Nation shall not take up
> Sword against nation;
> They shall never again know war. (Isaiah 2:4)

The book of Deuteronomy commands us with special emphasis: *Tzedek tzedek tirdof*, "Justice, justice shall you pursue, that you may thrive and occupy the land that [Adonai] your God is giving you" (16:20).

This messianic vision of peace and justice is at the heart of Judaism itself. We American Reform Jews have striven for more than a century to build coalitions of decency with peoples of all faiths, traditions, and backgrounds to make our country more just and compassionate, more peaceful. Zionism too was based in part upon the moral power of these prophetic principles. These shared values are among the strongest bonds that we American Jews have with the founding generation of Israeli Jews as well as with much of Israel today.

The prophetic voice spoke powerfully to the conscience of the builders of the modern State of Israel, reminding them that creating a Jewish state is justified only when the vision of the prophets is realized and institutionalized as the way of the nation. Israel's founders believed that the State of Israel could never exist for its own sake alone.

Israel's mission, our mission, is to embody peace, justice, and compassion.

David Ben-Gurion said, "History did not spoil us with power, wealth, a broad and a large amount of territory. However, it did grant us the uncommon intellectual and moral virtue[s], and thus it entitles and obligates us to be an *or la-goyim*, 'a light to the nations.'"[2]

Israel has been victorious in every war and has thrived in many fields of endeavor. This is a record of accomplishment that exceeds every other nation in the world, except perhaps the United States. That befits the purpose of Israel: to inspire people everywhere.

Chaim Nachman Bialik, the Hebrew national poet, put it this way as he prepared to tour the United States and raise money for the Jewish settlement in Palestine in 1926:

> Everything depends on how we live in our land and how we behave here. Our brethren in the Diaspora want to see here what is missing there in the cultural and spiritual and moral life of Galut [Diaspora].... If they do not feel that our values here are unwavering, we will not find a path to their hearts.... *Eretz Yisrael* [the Land of Israel] must give the Diaspora something more than Jews of any other country can give: something with a spirit of holiness, above and beyond the usual and commonplace.[3]

Can we say Israel has lived up to Bialik's expectations and dreams?

In many ways, yes! Israel is a thriving democracy. It has absorbed millions of Jews from around the world. It has built great universities, hospitals, and a thriving modern culture. It has the most powerful military in the Middle East. It is a world center of innovation in medical, communications, and environmental technologies, pharmaceuticals, computer software development, and startup companies of every kind. And despite the political instability of the region, Israel's economy is healthy (though there's much poverty among certain segments of the population, particularly the ultra-Orthodox and Arab sectors) and attracts investment from international companies and businesses.

But Israel today isn't a source of pride and inspiration for a large portion of your peers and younger American Jews as it was for my generation of baby boomers and my parents' and grandparents' generations. What's happened? Part of the answer has to do with what America has become for Jews. Here we are the beneficiaries of a vibrant, safe, multicultural society that respects religious and minority rights. We are among the most politically and economically successful and powerful Jewish communities in Jewish history.

American Jewish scholarship is prolific. Religious communities are thriving. Jewish schools, university studies departments, and adult learning opportunities are everywhere. There's more parity between Israeli and American Jewish communities today than there once was.

Many young Jews, in your generation and older, no longer feel they need Israel as a safe haven against anti-Semitism or even as an anchor for their Jewish cultural identity. Many feel that Israel has taken them for granted, that their loyalty is to expected but their voice is not heard by Israel or by organized American Jewish community leadership.

Changing the Zionist Crisis Narrative

In contrast to your generation's experience, I was born a year after the State of Israel was established and I was raised on the "crisis narrative" of Jewish history. The Holocaust hovered as a shadow over my childhood and taught Jews that when we're powerless, we're vulnerable to destruction. The Soviet Jewry movement of the 1960s warned us not to be naïve and make the same mistake our parents' generation made relative to threats against the lives of the Jews of Europe in the '30s and '40s.

By the time I was seventeen, Israel had fought three wars of self-defense. When I was twenty-three and living in Israel, the Jewish state was almost overtaken in the Yom Kippur War.

I was raised with the understanding that Israel couldn't afford to lose a single war and it had to have the strongest military and be the smartest nation in the Middle East, with a qualitative military and technological edge over other Middle Eastern nations.

Since 1948 Israel's survival has been the number-one priority for Israelis and world Jewry, at least up through my generation. Three words have driven our politics and fears: Security. Security. Security.

We come to this crisis mode honestly. After all, we Jews are a traumatized people from experiences ancient and modern. Our wounds are deep and our memories are long. Our closets are filled with ghosts of anti-Semites past. Our enemies are real—Iran, Hamas, Hezbollah, and ISIS are foes committed to Israel's destruction and to the murder of Jews. The Boycott, Divestment, Sanctions (BDS) movement, an international delegitimization movement, is also real, and it's unclear what Palestinian statehood really means. Will it be a threat or an opportunity?

To ignore any of these real threats is irresponsible. There should be no surprise that security remains a high priority for Israel and is the defining issue in Israeli politics and life.

At the same time, we Jews are also an eternally hopeful people. Optimism is built into our DNA. Despite our dangerous foes, we yearn for normality, to live peacefully and securely among the nations of the world. We don't want to argue constantly that our people has a right to exist when there's no such expectation of other nations.

The crisis narrative isn't a false model. It's based in reality and has served to unify world Jewry and propel us to activism on Israel's behalf. But despite this the crisis model is no longer adequate by itself to assure your generation's loyalty and commitment to the Jewish state.

You are less worried, rightly or wrongly, about overt military threats and delegitimization and are more concerned with social justice and the treatment of those on the periphery of Israeli society: the poor, Ethiopians, Arabs, women, immigrant workers, the Bedouin, and African asylum-seekers. For you the crisis model fails to provide a compelling narrative about why Israel ought to be central in our lives as Jews, beyond its mere survival.

It seems that you will support Israel as long as Israel embodies higher Jewish values. You aren't alone. Many young Israelis are also frustrated, demanding that their government and its policies embody higher Jewish values. Israelis want social justice, just as American Jews do and always have.

We Need a Conversation Focused on Values, Not Security

I agree that what we need now is a values-based conversation about Israel that differs from the crisis narrative that dominated the past six-plus decades.

A values-based conversation asks what it will take to address Israel's challenges and build a moral and just society whose policies reflect those values, our tradition, and our experience as a people. This conversation is about us as Jews, and it requires Israelis and American Jews to be partners in building the future of the Jewish people.

In a crisis-driven narrative, how minorities are treated is unlikely to even be addressed unless those minorities are regarded as a threat to Israel's survival or as a propaganda weapon for Israel's opponents. In a values-based conversation, the way a Jewish society relates to its minorities is an independent question that commands attention.

The crisis-driven conversation always returns to the measures the Israeli government and military need to repel the dangers Israel faces and the concrete responses of Israel to any given threat. It's concerned with the Iron Dome, smart bombs, blockades, targeted assassinations, security fences, Iran-funded terrorism, Hezbollah and Hamas tunnels, BDS, and the International Criminal Court.

But the values-driven conversation goes further, asking what should be done *after* a morally responsible Jewish nation chooses its means of defense. What should life under Israeli governance look like then? How can justice emerge?

My friend Yossi Klein Halevi, a journalist and writer who is a senior fellow at the Shalom Hartman Institute in Jerusalem, teaches that two passages in the Hebrew Bible embrace these concerns. Each begins with the admonition *zachor*, remember. The first is in Exodus: "You were strangers in the land of Egypt" (22:20). The second is in Deuteronomy: "Remember what Amalek did to you on your journey, after you left Egypt" (25:17). The first passage reminds us to avoid becoming cruel, because we Jews have ourselves been the object of cruelty from Egyptian enslavement and throughout history. The second reminds us not to be naïve, because when Amalek attacked our people from behind, his intent was to destroy us.

Halevi notes that Passover is the holiday when we are called upon to avoid becoming cruel even in victory and especially toward our enemies. Purim is the holiday when we're reminded not to be naïve and that security is of primary concern, lest our enemies succeed in their goals.

Today both Israel and the American Jewish community embrace traditional Jewish streams: compassion on the one hand, suspicion on the other. Both are authentic Jewish responses, and civility within our community is necessary to maintain our common purpose as a people and a nation.

Thankfully, many Israelis take seriously the tension between Israel's humanitarian concerns and its security demands. There are no easy answers when navigating through these conflicting concerns. We sitting here in America need to understand this and not presume that we know best and that somehow Israel has sacrificed its morality. It isn't true.

If we help shift the conversation from crisis mode to values mode, a new Zionist paradigm will emerge. We have had Herzl's political Zionism, Ahad Ha'am's cultural Zionism, Rav Kook's religious Zionism, Ze'ev Jabotinsky's and Menachem Begin's revisionist Zionism, and Avigdor Lieberman's proto-fascist nationalist Zionism. Dr. Tal Becker, also of the Shalom Hartman Institute in Jerusalem, suggests a new kind of Zionism: "aspirational Zionism."

Aspirational Zionism asks these questions:

- How do Jewish values augment Israel's democratic and pluralistic society?
- How do the moral aspirations of the biblical prophets and the compassionate impulse of the rabbinic sages help Israel face contemporary ethical challenges?
- How do Jews in Israel and around the world fight the sinister intentions of enemies bent on our destruction without sacrificing our moral sensibilities?
- How do we as a people genuinely pursue peace as a moral and quintessentially Jewish obligation in spite of the threat of war?
- How do we support our Israeli brothers and sisters while also advocating on behalf of the equal rights and dignity of Israel's minorities?

It's distressing that successive governments in Israel, operating in crisis mode, have set aside many pressing moral issues. When questioned about the urgency of these other issues, they argue that the current crisis necessarily dictates the choices the government and security forces make. Security eclipses all.

Ironically, it seems that the Jewish world's obsession with a crisis-based approach is creating its own crisis. The lack of sufficient attention to values is alienating too many Jews and is harming Israel's image and legitimacy on the world stage. Israel's supporters often say that if only people knew the truth about Israel's human rights record, its vibrant democracy, and its commitment to developing nations, then people would understand and become less critical and more supportive and proud. But they also don't engage in the values-based discussion of whether that record is adequate or how they might bring justice to a much wider swath of the country's minorities.

You Can Help Drive This Conversation—and You Must

Many believe it's not our place as American Jews to criticize Israel unless we're going to live there, pay taxes, and put our bodies and the bodies of our children on the line in its defense. I disagree. Yes, Israelis are the ones who live directly with the consequences of their government's decisions. However, everything Israel does affects us here, for better or worse. Israel's values influence *our* values. Its communal standing affects *our* safety and security. We're involved. To suggest that we remain quiet is contrary to our self-interest and our role as *ohavei am Yisrael u-M'dinat Yisrael*, lovers of the Jewish people and the State of Israel.

The State of Israel belongs to the entire Jewish people, and it matters to all of us. Rather than walking away in disgust and frustration, you can change the conversation and exert your influence. You need Israel, and Israel needs you and your sensibilities—your outrage, your energy, your creativity, your compassion, your sense of justice. Please know this. You *can* change the terms of the discussion. If you don't try, we all will lose, as will your children and your children's children.

Love,
Dad

Part IV

Living and Sustaining a Good Life

Metrics for Measuring Your Life

Dear Daniel and David:

I was only nine when my father died, so from a very early age I felt I was on my own, even though my mother was a strong, loving presence in my life.

She did her best, but she couldn't be everything to my brother and me. We had to fill in the holes, taking our lumps, picking ourselves up when we fell, and going on as best we could.

In my early twenties I began to seek out mentors, people older and wiser who lived their lives with dignity, integrity, and purpose. I looked for wisdom wherever I could find it—in teachers, friends, literature, art, history, psychology, the sciences, religious and mystical writings, Jewish community, social justice work, and politics.

When I finally reached the age my father had been when he died—exactly fifty-three years, seven months, and eleven days old—I felt a combination of relief, guilt, and fear. I never expected to live so long. My dad had his first heart attack when he was only 42 years old and, as a physician himself with a sub-speciality in cardiology working in the 1950s, he knew that he would not live to see my brother and me grow to adulthood. I thought about what it must have been like for him to know he was going to die and never see my brother and me grow up. I imagined being him reflecting on who I'd been, the people I'd loved, my accomplishments, and the values that had shaped me.

I wondered, if I died right then, at the same age he did, who could I say I was? How had I lived? Who was really important to me? Had I accomplished what I had hoped to up to that point? I even wondered how I'd make a case for myself before the Heavenly Judge as my soul was preparing to enter eternity, and what others would say about my life, character, heart, and soul.

I have considered many measures of who and what I've become. I have thought about the character of my faith; my respect and care for our family, friends, and community; and my advocacy for goodness, justice, compassion, and peace. I've also looked outside my own frame of reference and compared my values and priorities with those of the ancient sages—something I highly recommend as a means of shaking off your habitual perspective and seeing your life afresh. Much of the writing that speaks to us from the past resonates surprisingly well with a modern understanding of human nature.

I was surprised—and fascinated—to see that none of my own priorities for a life well lived was among the top seven measures the Talmudic sages believed would be of major interest to the heavenly tribunal (which you could think of as your higher self evaluating the choices you have made in your life). But I've drawn great inspiration and guidance from their thought-provoking "metrics" for our lives, and I think you will as well. Self-examination will make you each a better person than you already are. As all of us get older, feeling the touch of mortality more distinctly, I know the impulse to look inward and take stock grows stronger. As you follow it, I hope you'll consider these ancient questions that I've found so useful.

Question 1: Were You Honest in Business?

According to the Talmudic sage Raba, the first question the heavenly tribunal will ask us when we pass from this world is simply *Nasata v'natata b'emunah*, "Did you deal honestly and faithfully with people in your business practices?" (*Shabbat* 31a).

The starting point isn't "Were you respectful of your parents?" or "Did you love your kids?" or "Did you build a life about which you are proud?" It's not "Did you support good causes?" It's focused on our business practices, how we handled money. Did we have honest scales and balances, accurate weights and measures? Were we straightforward with our customers and clients? Did we pay our bills and taxes on time?

Why would Raba start here? Perhaps because Judaism understands all too well that it's human nature to look after number one first, to get all we can for ourselves. We all want our share. If we can't have it, then the tendency is to seek an advantage over others, even if it means cutting corners, lying, and deceiving—especially if we think we can get away with it. But if we can be impeccable here, in this most fraught arena, chances are we can navigate the rest of life more easily and honorably as well.

The Midrash says that "every human being dies with half their needs met" (*Kohelet Rabbah* 1:31), regardless of how much or how little we have. The question isn't whether we have enough or are comfortable enough, it's how honest and straight up we have been—and some of our greatest tests come in the realm of money.

Question 2: Did You Make Time for Your Spiritual Life?

The second question isn't surprising to me as a rabbi, but many Jews wouldn't have placed it anywhere near the top of their list, if it made it onto the list at all: *Kava'ata itim l'Torah*, "Did you set aside time for Torah?" (*Shabbat* 31a).

Rebbe Nachman of Breslov, one of our most brilliant and creative rabbinic geniuses, taught his disciples that they should study Torah at least four hours every day. But that was in a time when young boys spent their *lives* learning Torah. Most of us don't do that today; Torah learning hasn't been a priority for most liberal Western Jews. Most Jews I know don't set aside time regularly to study once a week, every two weeks, or even monthly.

Even fifteen hundred years ago, Raba understood how easy it is for busy people to dispense with Torah learning, rationalizing that it has only marginal value in their lives. Yet we are the "People of the Book." Torah is and always has been the epicenter of Jewish identity, and the way Jews have nurtured the heart, mind, and soul. The Torah, which is among the oldest texts in the world, is the formative moral, ethical, and spiritual force in Jewish life. It's an important pathway to God. Even if we are nonbelievers, Torah has been the central source helping Jews perpetuate, preserve, and enrich our collective Jewish memory.

I interpret Raba today as urging us to make time to strengthen our connection to our tradition, history, ethics, and faith. When we neglect this aspect of our lives, we lose our connection with our identity. We become marginal Jews at best—Jews with amnesia, out of touch with what has made us who we are, unable to survive as a people. The Torah feeds us, whether we read it for its history, poetry, or insights into what makes us who we are.

Question 3: Did You Busy Yourself with Creation?

Raba's third question also focuses on Jewish continuity: *Asakta b'friyah u'riviyah*, "Did you busy yourself with procreation?" (*Shabbat* 31a).

For many Jews today, that inquiry hits a raw nerve because not every Jew has kids. Some in our community are deeply sad and regretful about it, while others never wanted children to begin with. But the underlying issue Raba poses is far broader than parenting. You could rephrase his question to ask, "What's your legacy? How have you influenced and touched others? In what ways have you changed your community? Have you assured the continuity of our people, tradition, and values?"

These are the basic questions of Jewish life, and there are many ways to answer them. The gifts we bring to our families, our communities, and the world are highly individual. Assuring the continuity of our people might mean fighting climate change to some, and becoming a foster parent or advocating on behalf of Jewish people to others. It's up to you to determine what your legacy will be. But Raba reminds us that our lives are large, and each of us is responsible for creating something lasting, something that will ripple through time and feed those who come next. In your time on earth, he asks, were you busy planting seeds?

Question 4: Were You Hopeful?

In its traditional phrasing, Raba's fourth question is classically religious and doesn't, on the surface, seem particularly relevant to modern life: *Tzipita li'yeshuah*, "Did you expect salvation?" (*Shabbat* 31a). In other words, did you believe in the coming of the Messiah at the end of days?

But viewed more broadly, this fundamental rabbinic doctrine of faith in the future affirms hope, and that's the deeper question that speaks to liberal Jews today—are we hopeful?

There are many times when hope seems dim, when we want to throw up our hands and succumb to circumstances and despair. The truth is that if you live long enough, you'll suffer loss of all kinds. Your heart will break. The people you love will get sick and die. You'll get sick yourself, and sometimes illness will threaten your life. You'll lose a job or suffer financial setbacks. Your parents will get old and infirm. Your children will stumble and fall, and you'll feel powerless to help them. It will seem that you have been dealt a bad hand and there's nothing you can do about it.

But Rebbe Nachman of Breslov, who himself suffered from depression, teaches that perspective is everything, and that being joyful is a religious duty. It's forbidden, he writes, to despair!

Viktor Frankl, a Holocaust survivor and the author of *Man's Search for Meaning*, notes that he learned the most important truth in his life in the concentration camps, that "the last and greatest human freedom is the freedom to choose your attitude in any given set of circumstances, to choose one's own way."[1]

Tzipita li'yeshuah isn't so much about salvation in the world to come. It's a challenge to each of us to maintain a life-affirming attitude, to have the strength to shift our thinking and attitude, and to focus on the half-full glass. It's a challenge to step away from playing the victim, thinking only about what's wrong, worrying about when the other shoe will drop, and wondering who is out to get us next. Staying positive and hopeful may be the most difficult challenge we ever have to face. Raba teaches that we'll be measured in heaven—or can measure our own lives—by how well we try.

Questions 5 and 6: Did You Seek Wisdom and Learn to Discern What's True and What's False?

Raba's fifth and sixth questions continue to focus on what ought to be our priorities: *Pilpalta b'chochmah*, "Did you seek wisdom?" and *V'havanta davar mitoch davar*, "Were you able to understand/discern one thing from another?" (*Shabbat* 31a).

He isn't asking about our IQs. Rather, he's talking about our powers of observation, our capacity for differentiating between true and false and right and wrong, as well as our ability to be critical and self-critical. In a way I believe he's talking about our ability to see the impact of even our smallest actions and understand their cumulative power. It's a kind of everyday wisdom that's as profound as any great proclamation or grand insight.

When you boys were young, I took you with me to the supermarket to do the family's shopping. We always went to this market, and we spent a great deal of money there. And every time I passed by the yogurt-covered almonds, I'd reach in and grab one and put it in my mouth, not thinking anything of it. But you, Daniel, at the age of five, stopped me and said, "Daddy, did you pay for that?"

Oh my God, I thought. *I'm teaching my son that it's okay to steal.*

I immediately said, "No, Daniel, I didn't. But I'm going to do so, and I'm not going to do that again. I promise you!"

I've kept that promise. Children pay attention less to what we parents and teachers say than to what we do—which they watch very closely.

The power of the small is emphasized in the rabbinic commentary on a particular word in the book of Genesis, a word representing the human behavior that provoked God to unleash the legendary flood during Noah's days (Genesis 6:11). The word, *hamas*, appears only in this story in the Hebrew Bible and nowhere else, which made it difficult for the rabbinic commentators to define it precisely. Some said that the word connotes murder. Others said that it refers to sexual crimes. But the accepted interpretation is that it means theft—not on the level of grand larceny, but the pettiest of thefts, theft of an item less than a *p'ruta*, the smallest coin in the rabbinic era.

The Torah says that God brought the great flood because of this very small crime. The problem was that everyone was committing it, so when people went to the market and picked just one grape (or yogurt-covered almond) and ate it without paying for it, all the available food was stolen, distrust between customer and seller broke down, and civilization crumbled. Late-eighteenth-century philosopher Immanuel Kant calls this the "categorical imperative."

As you each make the small choices that define your larger life, ask, "Will this be good or bad for civilization?" That may sound grandiose, but our actions ripple and compound. If everyone curses, language suffers. If political candidates call each other liars and cheats, trust between our leaders and the public is shattered.

Everything we do matters. Knowing that, Raba asks, "Are we being honest and kind? Is what we are inside an accurate reflection of what we appear to be to others?"

One of my favorite teachers in rabbinical school was Dr. Abraham Zygelboim (z"l), a Talmudist at Hebrew Union College–Jewish Institute of Religion in Los Angeles. Dr. Zygelboim was a survivor of the Holocaust whose brother escaped to London and burned himself alive on the steps of Parliament to awaken the world to the catastrophe that was befalling his people. Dr. Zygelboim knew suffering, and he knew Talmud well, but it wasn't his Talmud teaching that left the biggest mark on me—it was one tiny, human action.

In the middle of the academic year, when I was twenty-five years old, I broke up with a young woman I believed was the love of my life. I was hurting badly, and between classes I needed time alone. I walked outside the college's building near the University of Southern California campus and seeing an out-of-the-way wall, I slid down, sat on the pavement, and cried. Out of nowhere Dr. Zygelboim came to me and kissed my forehead. He didn't say a word.

Dr. Zygelboim taught me more in that brief moment than all the Talmud I ever learned from him. He was kind, and that kindness was my greatest teacher.

The more wisdom and discernment you develop in your life, I believe, the more you will value kindness. For years I have been aware of a quote ascribed to Rabbi Abraham Joshua Heschel that affirms this position: "When I was young I admired clever people. Now that I'm old, I admire kind people."[2]

Question 7: Have You Been True to Yourself?

Raba's final question is based on a story from the Talmud: "Before his death, Rabbi Zusya said, 'In the coming world, they will not ask me, 'Why were you not Moses?' They'll ask me, 'Why were you not Zusya?'"[3]

In the end the question asked of each of us is simple: "Have you been true to yourself, doing that which you were meant to do, and did you do your best with what you were given?"

Zusya understood that he had to be Zusya, not Moses.

Being ourselves and no one else isn't always easy. We admire certain people, and at times we may envy their gifts and talents, wishing that they were our own. I confess I often wish that I had an additional ten or twenty IQ points and that I had grown up in Israel, speaking Hebrew as my first language; that I could speak Yiddish, play golf like Tiger, and sing like Sinatra. As a spiritual person, I wish I could hear God's voice as did the biblical prophets Jeremiah, Isaiah, and Micah. And if I could, I'd have the brilliance, decency, poetic spirit, and religious vision of Rabbi Abraham Joshua Heschel.

I know, however, that I'm not smarter than I am, nor do I have the same gifts as Tiger, Sinatra, Isaiah, or Heschel.

Yet never has there been anyone exactly like me, or exactly like you. If we spend our lives yearning to be someone else, who will be me and who will be you? The greatest bit of wisdom we can learn is how to accept ourselves as unique and empowered to make an impact in the world as only we can do. That's where we have to begin as we build our lives as works of art that make a contribution, that touch and change lives.

Phil Rosenthal, a member of our community, is an especially smart, funny, and kind man. He's beloved in the entertainment industry not just because of his talent but also because of his heart.

Phil was executive producer of the television comedy *Everyone Loves Raymond*, and he's created a new PBS show called *I'll Have What Phil's Having!*, in which he travels to his favorite cities in the world and seeks out the best food he can find. He's not a chef, but he loves good food, good ethnic food, good inexpensive food, and he wants his audience to share the joy that he has in seeking out the best meals in any city.

Phil showed an episode of *I'll Have What Phil's Having!* to my congregation. In the question-and-answer period afterward, one man asked him, "Tell us—you don't cook yourself, but you're doing a show about cooking. Why?"

Phil's answer was Zusya's answer. "Some people," he said, "are chefs and they're really good at it. I can't cook, but I can appreciate their cooking. They can't write a sitcom, which is what I know how to do. Everyone has to do what they know how to do, and we all ought to be able to appreciate that and celebrate them and their gifts."

We have so little time. Four score years and ten, if we're lucky. That seems like an eternity when we're young, but when we get older, it's very brief. You guys are now young adults, yet only recently you were so small that I could carry each of you with your head in my palm and your body lying on one of my arms. Now one of you is 5 feet 11 inches and the other 6 feet 2 inches.

Time races. Make the most of your precious lives. And always ask the one question from the book of Deuteronomy that rests at the center, the core of Raba's seven questions: *Uvacharta bachayim*, "Are you choosing life?" (30:19).

That question means everything. How will you answer?[4]

Love,
Dad

Redefining Success

Dear Daniel and David:

It's easy—and natural—to get swept up in the prevailing aspirations of the moment. If I asked each of you what it means to be successful, for example, you might say something about having a good job—something with a good income and that commands the esteem of others. That sounds like success to many of your peers and mine.

Going a step further, I might ask whether you could be happy and have a sense of meaning if you *didn't* have that kind of success. In other words, must you have the good job, high income, and status to have a meaningful life? What's essential for you to be happy and fulfilled?

These are the kinds of questions you are not pressed to consider when you have the high-profile job and comfortable paycheck, or when you are striving for them alongside everyone else. But they can gnaw at you if you have made different choices or suspect that another sort of life would be a better fit. We often tend to set our lives in motion and let them unfold without pausing to reflect until events give us reason to question where we have placed our time and energy. So I think it's useful to step outside the assumptions and the career juggernaut occasionally to ask whether the life you are working for is the one you want, and whether the priorities you have chosen actually reflect who you are and want to be.

I've been thinking lately about how different kinds of people find such meaning. For instance, I was fascinated at the sorts of questions that came up for a young woman I know when her best friend challenged her direction. I've also been interested in how a near-death experience rejiggered a businessman's perspective about what's really important. And because I'm never far from the thinking of the sages, I've looked in on what they have to say about the question of what truly makes us wise, strong, rich, and respected—qualities that might add up to fulfillment in our lives.

No one can answer for us the ongoing question of how we should use our talents, live our lives, and feed our hungry souls. But in sharing our stories, questions, and insights about each other, I hope we can keep each other company in our search.

Whose Definition of Success Counts? Your Best Friend's?

At thirty years old, Gabrielle, a member of my congregation, seemed deeply contented with her life as a Hollywood production assistant and with her boyfriend, Matthew, with whom she was falling in love. But she sought me out after a disturbing conversation with her closest childhood friend that called her values and choices into question.

Gabrielle's friend Leslie had moved to New York, and when she dropped into town for the first time in a year, Gabrielle eagerly met her for drinks. Topic A was Matthew.

"So what does Matthew do for a living?" Leslie asked as soon as they sat down.

"He's a fifth-grade teacher in the Los Angeles public schools."

"Oh my God. Really? Is *that* what he wants to do with his life?"

"Yes," Gabrielle said. "He loves kids. They love him, and he loves being a teacher!"

"But a *schoolteacher*? In those crumbling public schools?" Leslie said. "That's kind of a red flag, isn't it? He'll never make any money, and I know you won't be happy just scraping by with him! I know you like him, but you can do so much better than that."

"Wait," Gabrielle said, taken aback. "He's smart and generous and funny and kind, and you're saying that unless he's a CEO of a Fortune-500 company making a million dollars a year, he's not worth my time and I won't be happy with him?"

"Absolutely," Leslie said. "It's as easy to love a rich man as a poor one, and there are plenty of smart, generous, funny CEOs out there. Why do you want to suffer?"

Gabrielle shook her head as she recounted the conversation. "I don't know why that hit me so hard," she told me. "She hasn't even met him and she was so dismissive. But now I wonder if she's right, and maybe I'm just being a stupid romantic instead of thinking about what kind of life we'd really be able to give our kids with jobs like ours."

I looked at the young woman I'd known for so many years—through her childhood in the Temple's schools, her bat mitzvah and Confirmation, her first forays into adult life. She'd been glowing since she met Matthew, and from what she'd told me, they were a beautifully matched couple.

"Gabrielle, I think your friend's priorities and values are mixed up," I told her. "It sounds to me like Matthew is a terrific guy in all the ways you want and need. You have enough life experience to know your heart and what makes you happy with a man, and you say you have fallen in love with him in a way you have never done before with anyone else. I recommend that you ignore Leslie's comment, follow your heart, and see where your relationship with Matthew leads you."

"You don't think I should 'aim higher'?" she asked.

"Gabrielle," I said, "I know you and your family, and though your parents provided well for you and your sisters, money and job status were never the chief concerns in their lives, and I don't think they are in yours either. Your friend seems only to care about Matthew's income and status, and I don't believe that those are what make for a successful and happy relationship. Besides, being a teacher is a noble profession, even if it's not the most lucrative. For a person to commit himself to educating young people is worthy of everyone's respect. If you're concerned about your total family income, remember that if you marry him you're likely going to need to work as well, and that's two incomes. Who knows what Matthew will decide to do in five or ten years. He may remain a teacher or move to a different position with a different income."

Jobs and careers change, I told her. But the things she valued in Matthew—his love for people, his generous heart, the way his rhythms and temperament matched hers—were what she'd hungered for in her life and in her relationship with a partner. On her personal scale of values, didn't her love for Matthew and the people they were together eclipse any arbitrary standard Leslie was trying to impose?

It can be disconcerting to realize that in following what we love, we have diverged from the paths and expectations of our old friends or others whose opinions we value. But sometimes in seeing our choices challenged we have a chance to consciously review what's important to us and to reconfirm for ourselves that they still feel valid and alive. Sarah didn't have to think long. Her heart knew the answer to every question she brought me.

Success will come to both Gabrielle and Matthew, I predict, not as a result of chasing it or following anyone's formula for achieving it, but as an outgrowth of encouraging each other to follow their souls' passions. It won't look like Leslie's version of success—it will be richly their own. As Viktor Frankl puts it, "Don't aim at success—the more you aim at it and make it a target, the more you are going to miss it. For success, like happiness, cannot be pursued; it must ensue … as the unintended side effect of one's dedication to a cause greater than oneself."[1]

You each might want to ask, what *does* success look like to me? How will I recognize it in myself and my partner? What am I dedicated to in my life that's greater than myself? What makes me happy?

The View from When Time Runs Out

For most of us, even those as old as I am, it can seem as though there will be plenty of time to pursue our true course and become the people we were meant to be. But it's easy to let currents of routine overtake our larger visions. That's why I appreciate the jolt of urgency that comes from people like Ric Elias, a businessman who was on U.S. Airways Flight 1549, the flight that famously touched down in the Hudson River on January 15, 2009.

As Elias tells the story on the TED stage, he was in seat 1D, close to the flight attendants at the front of the plane. Suddenly there were explosions in the engines and the cabin began to fill with smoke. The jet had hit a flock of geese and the engines sputtered and then shut down. Though the flight attendants had been casually reassuring at first, he could see their panic. He was certain he was going to die.

And then he got a second chance at life.

Walking off his miracle flight, Elias said, he realized he'd learned three important lessons:

1. Everything can change in an instant. "We all have a bucket list of things we want to do, the people we want to reach out to, the fences we need to mend, all the experiences we want to have but

haven't yet done." He reflected, "I learned not to postpone any-thing in my life."

2. He had allowed his ego too often to drive him and get in his way, so he had wasted time on things that didn't matter with peo-ple who did matter—for instance, arguing with loved ones. He decided, he said, to eliminate all negative energy from his life. "I no longer choose to be right, to always have to have the final word"; rather, he chooses to step back and leave more room for others.

3. He learned that dying isn't as scary as he'd imagined. "It's almost as if we've been preparing for it all our lives," he said. Facing death, he realized how much he loved his wife and children, and how much he wanted to be the best spouse, friend, and father he could be.[2]

Having seen into the future that would exist without him, Elias feels he's been given a chance to come back and live his life differently, to take the new start he's been given and begin again. I believe all of us can do that, no near-disaster necessary. As you think about what you really want, what makes you happy, and what success means, why not review your life as Elias did and each ask yourself these questions:

- What would I change about my life if I could?
- What is important to get done now that I have put off?
- Whom do I truly want to spend my time with, and how might I change and deepen my relationships with the people I really care about?
- How can I begin doing these things now?

Life *can* change in an instant. What would happen if you decided not to postpone the changes you long to make and become the person you long to be? What would happen if you decided to satisfy the wants and hun-gers of your life now?

Wisdom, Strength, Riches, and Respect: An Ancient Perspective on Fulfillment

I think it's reasonable to guess that if we could lead our lives in a way that allowed us to be wise, strong, rich, and respected, we might be able to say we were somewhat—or perhaps extremely—fulfilled. These four worldly attributes would seem to satisfy the requirements for modern success in many fields. So you'll probably be interested to know that the insights I share with you now are from the second-century Palestinian sage Ben Zoma, not a twenty-first-century leadership guru.

I've been circling and circling and circling the question of what makes a successful and fulfilling life, and I think Ben Zoma comes to that theme in an illuminating way with these questions:

Eizeh hu chacham? Who is wise?

Eizeh hu gibor? Who is strong [or heroic]?

Eizeh hu ashir? Who is rich?

Eizeh hu m'chubad? Who is respected? (*Pirkei Avot* 4:1)

His answers give us a fascinating, deeply human view of what it might look like to live as the embodiment of those virtues. I love them for the way their truth runs counter to the prevailing expectations of his time, and ours.

Who is wise?

We might presume that the wise person is the smartest one in the room, the one who is graced with a high IQ and much education. But no, Ben Zoma says that the wise person is *halomed mi kol adam*, the one who is humble, curious, open-hearted, and willing to learn something from every human encounter, regardless of the other person's intelligence, achievements, worldliness, station, wealth, or occupation.

It's as if Ben Zoma is saying that high intelligence isn't necessarily destiny, nor are Ivy League degrees or the highest scores on the SAT, GRE, LSAT, or MCAT. None of that automatically confers wisdom, he says. The well-educated person who closed-mindedly, arrogantly, and hard-heartedly dismisses the thoughts, experiences, and opinions of other people is actually, according to Jewish values, the opposite of wise—that man or woman is a fool. The wise person is one who can hear and absorb the wisdom that comes from others.

Dr. Elisabeth Kübler-Ross tells the story of how she became distressed in her work with dying patients because she didn't feel she was really reaching them. One evening she returned to visit a man dying of cancer, and as she approached his room she overheard him pouring out his heart to someone she couldn't see from where she stood in the hall.

Kübler-Ross was stunned because this man had never opened up that way with her. She waited for the conversation to conclude and for his remarkable counselor, whoever she was, to come out so she could learn how she'd connected so powerfully with him. Moments later the cleaning lady walked into the hall.

"How did you get him to talk so freely?" Kübler-Ross asked.

"Honey, I didn't do a thing. I guess he just knew I was willing to listen. And when he started to talk I just sat there, held his hand, and listened to him. The good Lord did all the rest."[3]

I tell all the children in our synagogue schools that the reason God gave us two ears and one mouth is so that we'll listen more and talk less. The wise person lives this truth, listens well, asks pertinent questions, and refrains from self-referencing. It's a demonstration of wisdom to respect and honor the one standing before you. You treat each person with patience and empathy, withholding judgment and knowing you have nothing to prove.

The wise person, I believe, doesn't ignore education. Of course we need to learn from the great thinkers, teachers, scientists, historians, and writers so we can gain from their insights and grow. Of course we have to acquire the skills necessary to do well whatever our particular calling demands of us. Still, the more one knows, the more one knows how little one knows. The Talmudic sage Eliezar said that though he had learned much Torah, what he knew was comparable only to what a "dog laps from the lake" (*Sanhedrin* 68a).

I've so often found that the most important life lessons—the ones that often ultimately lead to the greatest fulfillment—don't come from literature and enlightened writings but rather from family, friends, and my encounters with strangers.

Who is strong or heroic?

Ben Zoma's second question is *Eizeh hu gibor*, "Who is strong [or heroic]?" The answer again is the opposite of what we might expect. The strong or heroic person isn't the one with the most intellectual heft, physical prowess, or emotional forcefulness. Though the warrior, the 350-pound NFL lineman, the powerful business executive, the intimidating litigator, the winning politician, or the acclaimed celebrity may have used their requisite physical, intellectual, and emotional attributes to win the day, Ben Zoma doesn't believe that their strength comes from how well they can muster those qualities on behalf of their own interests or the interests of others. Rather, Ben Zoma's idea of strength and heroism has to do with self-control.

Eizeh hu gibor? Hakovesh et yitzro. "Who is strong? The one who controls his *yetzer*."

The *yetzer* is difficult to define, but it involves our impulses, passions, and drives—jealousies, pride, envy, anger, rage, ambition, competitiveness, acquisitiveness, and sexual appetite. Each of these, when not controlled, can be destructive to us and hurtful to others. We see this happen all the time, and often it's the most talented, gifted, and brilliant among us who bring themselves down through their unmanaged base drives.

The Talmud warns, "The greater the person, the greater the *yetzer*" (*Kiddushin* 52b), and we all best beware.

When it comes to the *yetzer*, Walt Whitman writes in Song of Myself, "Logic and sermons never convince."[4] It's as though we're riding an elephant that's barreling through the forest, tearing down everything in its path. Facing, and stopping, the elephant is our most heroic act, Ben Zoma would argue.

My friend and colleague Rabbi Amy Eilberg puts it well when she writes that Ben Zoma "defines heroism as an inside job. The hero is one who attains a measure of success in learning his own interior landscape deeply enough to resist the powerful pull of long-practiced destructive habits."[5]

True Jewish heroism is about facing down and controlling the *yetzer hara* (literally, "the evil inclination"), the part of us that we prefer others never see and about whose unchecked actions we're likely to feel shame. Real strength is about taking control of those impulses, passions, and drives that demean us and others and transforming that unchecked energy toward positive ends.

This battle between our *yetzer tov* (literally, "good inclination") and our *yetzer hara* never ends. I imagine two little Johnnys sitting on my shoulders, whispering into my ears. One of them, the bad *yetzer*, eggs me on to do self-centered things for myself, and myself alone. "You deserve everything you crave and want," he says. "No holds barred—do it!" he commands. "Don't hold back! Take it! It's yours. You're entitled!"

The other little Johnny says, "Hold on there, bub! You know what's right and wrong. You know what's kind and decent. You know what's intemperate, selfish, and self-centered. Don't give in to that creep. He couldn't care less about what's in your best interest. Think instead about the other guy and understand yourself and your role in a situation! Do the right thing!"

That battle goes on inside of me often, as it does within everyone, and I know it will continue until the day I die. Judaism teaches that we will never eliminate the bad *yetzer*, unless we are a complete tzaddik, one of the thirty-six *lamed vavniks*, the truly pure and righteous souls that Jewish tradition teaches enable the world to survive.

For the rest of us, the bad *yetzer* is always there. It's a part of our nature as human beings, but we can control it, put it away, and act as if it holds little or no influence and power over us. That is our choice to make, and it's our choice alone. No one can compel us to do or say anything we know is morally compromising, destructive to ourselves, or unkind to others.

Who is rich?

Ben Zoma's third question is *Eizeh hu ashir*, "Who is rich?"

Most people think of wealth in terms of measuring things by the numbers. How much of this? How many of that? How big and expensive is it?

There's nothing wrong with doing that. Indeed, financial security and comfort are things we all want and need. The medieval Jewish philosopher Maimonides says that the well-being of the soul is obtained only after the well-being of the body is secure.[6] In contrast to certain ascetic religious traditions, Judaism has no particular attraction to poverty. We don't believe that there's anything noble in it. And surveys show the stress it brings can lead to bad health and even early death.

That being said, who among us is really ever satisfied? Isn't it the case with most of us that there's something we want even if we need nothing? That's why the answer to *Pirkei Avot*'s question, *Eizeh hu ashir*, "Who is rich?" seems obvious—the wealthy person is the one who has everything he or she wants.

The rabbis, however, disagreed. *Hasameach b'chelko*, the happy one isn't the one with much material wealth, but the one who is content or satisfied with whatever he or she has, even if it's meager. In this way the poor may be "wealthier" than the rich.

A wealthy friend confessed to me many years ago, "Everybody thinks I'm smart and worthy because I'm rich. But I'm not so smart, and I don't think I'm all that worthy. Yes, I worked hard, but no harder than a lot of people who didn't do nearly as well as me. I've just been lucky."

My friend, by the way, was both smart and worthy, and also very generous. But he was right that wealth often brings an added measure of respect and admiration that the wealthy person may or may not deserve but that comes his or her way only because people assume that the rich are smarter, work harder, and are the best at what they do. Often this assumption is right, but not always. Sometimes the wealthy are just lucky. They made the right investment or they inherited a fortune from their parents and grandparents through little or no effort of their own.

Unfortunately, of course, money doesn't address every need, and it brings with it its share of problems. There are many people who have much but are not at all happy or fulfilled. Though money enables us to do things we otherwise would never be able to do, and wealth gives us a measure of independence and latitude in our choices, it can't fill the holes in our hearts and souls that can only be filled up with love, friendship, meaningful work, engagement in worthy pursuits, and faith.

Judaism teaches that wealth is measured not relative to an external standard but relative to our inner virtues of humility, compassion, and generosity.

Who is respected?

The fourth question is *Eizeh hu m'chubad*, "Who is respected?"

Ben Zoma says that the respected person isn't necessarily the most successful with the most lucrative position and the most job promotions. Instead, he says, *ham'chubad hu ham'chabed et habriyot*, "The most respected and honorable person is the one who respects others"—regardless of their accomplishments, title, station, wealth, power, and renown.

The most honorable person looks past distinctions and treats every human being with kindness and respect, be he or she a pauper or royalty.

Taken together our second-century sage's definitions offer a vision of the fulfilled person as one who can learn something from everyone he or she meets, keep baser urges in check and listen to his or her better angels, be satisfied with whatever he or she has, and treat everyone with kindness and respect.

To me it would seem possible to look back, at the end of life, with a sense that one had lived well if these were the qualities that shone through one's actions and days. Sarah's boyfriend, Matthew, sounded like a man who'd be able to do so. So did Ric Elias who emerged from the downed jetliner.

How about you?

What Do We Crave and Seek, and What Is Our Purpose?

I know I began by asking each of you to think about how you define success, but I think the more important questions are these: What is it that your soul craves most dearly? What do you really seek? What's the deepest purpose for which you have come into the world?

Our lifelong task is to find the match between our gifts and the world's needs and, Ben Zoma might suggest, to help others do the same. Jewish tradition teaches that what's most important is not the dollars and material goods we have accumulated or the number of people over whom we preside, or even the deserved awards we have earned or been given.

What matters are the individuals we have helped to become their best selves, whom we have taught, nurtured, strengthened, healed, comforted, and loved.

Success, it seems, is best measured by the heart.

Love,
Dad

Creating Your Legacy

Dear Daniel and David:

> Lives of great [human beings] all remind us
>> We can make our lives sublime,
> And, departing, leave behind us
>> Footprints on the sands of time.[1]

So said Henry Wadsworth Longfellow in "A Psalm of Life," which so inspired me that I never forgot it.

There's a Jewish tradition that's related. It says we have three names. One is the name our parents gave us. The next is the name we are called by those who know us. And the third is the one we earn for ourselves. It's this third name, the one that resonates through time with the meaning of our days on earth, that I want to consider with you in this letter.

I know you are both young yet, with so much ahead of you, but how would you like to be remembered? What would people say of you if you died today? Would that "name" capture all you dreamed of being?

The Swedish chemist Alfred Nobel woke up one morning to see his obituary in the paper. It was a mistake—he'd been confused with his brother, who had died the day before—yet there were the achievements of his life laid out in black and white. Alfred, the obituary said, would be remembered as the inventor of dynamite, a man who had made his fortune by licensing to governments the use of this explosive for weapons. His invention, said the story, made it possible for nations to achieve new levels of mass destruction of armies and civilian populations.

Nobel was stunned to think of his name being forever associated with death and destruction. So he decided to change course, using his vast fortune to establish awards in a broad range of fields that serve humankind.

Implicit in Alfred Nobel's change of life-script was his recognition of the difference between personal success and personal *significance*. Though the obituary described him as a brilliant chemist (which he was), and though dynamite had been a breakthrough development in mining, construction, and engineering, he was struck by the negative impacts of his creation and he became determined to contribute something positive.

Today hardly anyone knows that Alfred Nobel developed dynamite. Instead, we remember him as the man who created awards to inspire the most brilliant and creative minds, hearts, and spirits of our time to serve our greatest human interests.

Defining Your Legacy with an Ethical Will

If you each were to write your own obituary, what would you say about yourself? How would you wish to be remembered by others? What lasting and meaningful contribution would you be proud to say has defined your purpose, goals, and life ends? If you could write a short message that would appear on your tombstone, what would that be? Would those who know you best agree that your chosen statement truly represents you?

To answer these questions is to probe the essence of who you understand yourself to be and what you care about most. But I believe there's an even more illuminating way to think about your life and legacy and to distill the wisdom you already possess into a form you can share with your loved ones far into the future. It's by following the Jewish custom of creating an ethical will, a document in which you bequeath the lessons of your lifetime, however long it is, to those who come after you.

The tradition of writing ethical wills began in biblical times. We find the very first example in the book of Genesis, when Jacob instructs his twelve sons from his deathbed and gives them directives and advice on their futures (49:1–33).

These directives gained particular importance between the twelfth and seventeenth centuries, when Jews suffered impoverishment and deprivation throughout Europe in ghettos and in the lands of dispersion as a result of the Spanish Inquisition. Having little in the way of material possessions to leave for their heirs, our people poured their essential selves into ethical wills. Most of these writings contain no lists of assets and property. Instead, to read them is to peer into the inner lives, hearts, minds, and souls of our ancestors. They tell us what was of ultimate value to them, what they cherished, what they felt about their families, what lessons they learned, and what acquired wisdom and truths they hoped to impart to their children and grandchildren.[2]

I think it would be extraordinarily valuable for each of you to revive this tradition for yourself. Because you don't yet have children, the ethical will you'd write today would be an exercise in distilling as concisely as you can what you believe and value most. There's an old saying, "If you want to know how to live your life, think about what you would like people to say about you after you die—and then live backward."

Thinking about the legacy we'd like to leave the people we love and care about most can help us keep straight our own priorities and even help chart the future. Carefully considering how you each want to be remembered allows you to formulate a kind of strategic plan for your life at any age. Nonprofit organizations, synagogues, and businesses develop mission statements; an ethical will is a kind of personal mission statement. As such it ought to articulate your own vision of what you are at your changeless core.

Viktor Frankl believed that he survived the concentration camps because he had important work he needed to complete. He notes that we don't in fact invent our missions as individuals. Rather, we seek to detect them, to uncover them, and then strive to fulfill them, much in the same way that Michelangelo is said to have remarked that he didn't create images out of stone but rather released what was trapped inside the marble.[3]

Is the Life You Have Chosen Enough?

Ever since Adam and Eve left the Garden of Eden, we humans have asked if our toil in living has meaning and value beyond our ability to make ends meet. Most of us want to know whether what we have spent our time doing has significance. We wonder if our tiny candles are bright enough to cast a measure of light or if they are too dim to be detected at the end of our days. We question if what we do and what we have done is good enough or if something greater is expected of us.

I remember speaking with a member of our community who by any standard is a success in life. He's a respected and revered leader, attorney, and thinker, and a wonderful, thoughtful mensch. He was complaining to me (as he has to his former law partners on many occasions, apparently without effect) that motivation for profit had become overly important in his firm, that partners' meetings had become primarily discussions about how to grow the firm, make more money, and attract more prestigious clients and cases. The firm wanted to engage the best and brightest young attorneys, but to do so would mean paying these twenty-six- and twenty-seven-year-old attorneys exorbitant salaries, higher than many of the incomes of people who'd worked hard for years for far more modest incomes.

For a number of years he'd been asking, "Why? Is this the reason we became attorneys?"

My friend didn't need a wake-up call himself because he couldn't care less about whether he'll be remembered as the lawyer who made a ton of money and won the biggest cases. He'd rather devote more of the firm's time to taking on pro bono work and doing well for people who can't afford attorneys.

But what if you were one of the young attorneys? Which of many competing values would guide you as you considered working for a premium salary in my friend's firm or choosing a more service-oriented path? In your changeless core, what's essential to you? What balance of giving and receiving feels right to you as you navigate your life?

These are difficult questions, but you already know the answers. You need only take time to reflect and realize what already lives within you, even if it's hidden away from yourself and others right now, and then articulate it as clearly as you can.

For many of us, the part of our soul that's hungry for meaning, that wants to know that our life matters and that the world is a little better for our having been here, is buried so deeply and obscured so much by life's traffic that we rarely focus enough on it to clean the slate and ask: Why am I here? What's my life's purpose? You may feel, as I so often do, that you haven't done enough, lived enough, learned enough, taught enough, prayed enough, given enough, created enough, or advocated enough to fully express that purpose. Yet each purposeful act we take has meaning.

Rabbi Abraham Joshua Heschel notes that the greatest challenge we face in our lives is to comprehend the ultimate meaning of this moment. Quoting from Psalms, he says, "How can I repay unto God all God's bountiful dealings toward me?" (116:12).

Rabbi Heschel suggests that when life itself is an answer, when we live our lives fully and well, seeking to bring some measure of compassion and comfort, peace and justice into the lives of others, then death is not an end but a homecoming.

An ethical will can help you live with such values in mind.

Writing to the Future

Jewish tradition doesn't have formal requirements about what should be written in an ethical will. Whatever we end up writing ought to reflect timeless and unchanging values and principles, regardless of the situations in which we might find ourselves at any particular moment in our lives. They should be written as if our circumstances never change—though we know they do—and should express principles that can withstand the loss of a job, home, or financial security; the disintegration of relationships, marriages, and friendships; and even the death of our beloved family and friends.

When you have children, your ethical will should convey to them the best of yourself and your hopes for the future.

As I read the treasure trove of ethical wills that has come down to us, I'm struck by what parents want to convey to their children and grandchildren. One dying parent instructed his child not to cut off relations with family when tensions arose between them. Another told his sons and daughters to avoid drinking and eating in excess, to stay away from gambling, and to avoid risky business ventures. A third instructed her children to refine their speech and avoid volcanic bursts of anger and mean-spiritedness. She wanted her children to speak respectfully to each other and others, and to be kind, charitable, and generous of heart always, not just some of the time.

A father counseled his sons to be honest in their business dealings, pay their debts on time, and avoid behavior that brings ill repute on the family's good name. Yet another urged his children and grandchildren to study some Torah every day of their lives, support the Jewish community generously, and look out for and take care of their fellow Jews.

Notably, some of these documents were written by people who didn't have children of their own but were leaving these instructions to their nieces, nephews, and people they mentored in business. You could do that too.

The ethical wills I've read are inspirational. Most of them weren't intended to produce guilt or to punish, blame, harass, or control a child or loved one from the grave. To the contrary, the vast majority were open-hearted and generous.

On the single occasion I've had to read a mother's ethical will at a funeral, I was moved by how deeply it touched all of us. The will had been written twenty years earlier and articulated what the woman believed, valued, and wanted her children and grandchildren to do with their lives, and how she wanted them to remember her. It was as if she were speaking to her loved ones in her own beautiful words from the other side.

I recommend that you, too, each give voice to your spirit and write your own ethical will now, when you are a young adult. Return to it every so often and consider whether you are living in a way that reflects your essential core and values. Think of the will as your individual strategic plan, but rather than focusing on material things, write about what you believe is important, who you are, what you cherish above all else, and what you would want people to believe about you. Then, when it's time, add words that speak to your children, and theirs.

I wish you a sublime life, full of meaning, wonder, and joy.

Love,
Dad

Why Optimism Is Better Than Pessimism

Dear Daniel and David:

We live in times of head-spinning change. In just the span of your lifetimes, we have seen the rise of the Internet age, ubiquitous computers and "smart" devices, paradigm-shifting discoveries in biotechnology, genetics, physics, and more. Our brightest minds have mapped the human genome and the surface of Mars, melded our bodies with machines, and proven the existence of dark matter. It's a stunning, inspiring time to be alive.

It's also, for many of us, a frighteningly bleak age. Our ties to each other, in our communities and the world, seem ever more fragile. Societies have been destabilized by such forces as terrorism since 9/11; the growth of radical fundamentalism in so many countries, including our own; violence; the movement of entire populations as refugees flee from war and terror; increasing fear and hatred of the other. Climate change is threatening life on the planet, and too many political leaders are in denial, turning away from actions that could help save us. The recession of 2009 and the financial losses suffered by millions of Americans devastated savings and hopes and dreams. And the coarsening of public discourse, culminating in the erratic and disturbing 2016 presidential campaign, signals an increasingly unsure future.

In the midst of this, the light and the darkness of our time, I think each of you can find out much about your values by considering a deceptively simple question: Are you an optimist or a pessimist?

Your answer is important because the way you feel, the nature of your outlook, and the way you behave as a result will shape not only what you believe but also how you live and how you and your peers confront challenges now and in the future.

Optimism and Pessimism, Freedom and Enslavement

You may remember the last time we talked about this question of optimism versus pessimism as a family. It was on the first night of Passover one year when, as we have for more than twenty-five years, we celebrated together in our home. As I do every year, I'd compiled, written, and edited our "Rosove Family Haggadah," a kind of living text that, like the Haggadot of old, evolves over time.

The traditional Haggadah is a library of prayers, poetry, and readings taken from multiple eras in Jewish history, going back to the biblical age. That makes it a mirror of the Jewish experience over time, encapsulated in the writings of our people's greatest prophets, sages, mystics, philosophers, activists, and thinkers overlaid by our people's core values that were developed over thirty-six hundred years in every land and age. I always imagine that when we engage with the Haggadah, we're sitting around the table with Moses, the rabbis of the Talmud, and every Jew around the world, transported beyond our time into Jewish memory.

Our family Haggadah, while it includes the core traditional passages, also borrows from other Haggadot that bring forward modern Jewish experience, as well as materials from outside the Jewish experience that reflect our people's universal values. The essential value at the heart of the Seder is that we have to fight cruelty wherever it occurs in the world, because we know the heart of the stranger. We have been there historically as a people. We were slaves to Pharaoh in Egypt, and some of us have experienced the cruelty of the oppressor personally. Tradition teaches that it's our duty as Jews never to forget who we are. Memory necessarily leads us to be activists on behalf of the freedom of every human being everywhere in the world.

We can never become complaisant and still fulfill our duty as Jews. That's the core value of Passover. I've made it a practice to include sidebar quotations and explanations of ritual, midrashim, and other material in our Haggadah that prompt us to discuss, debate, question, and reflect on our people's long historic legacy, that we might apply that thinking to what has taken place during the past year in our lives, our country, the State of Israel, and the broader non-Jewish world. On our holy day of freedom, we focus our conversation on the themes of enslavement, liberation, and redemption as a way to bring us back to our core Jewish values and what we hope for in the coming year.

That's how we happened upon the topic of optimism and pessimism that year. Just before the Maggid section, when we tell the story of the Exodus, I asked everyone to reflect on two statements, one by Harry S. Truman and the other by Nelson Mandela.

Truman said, "A pessimist finds difficulties in every opportunity; an optimist finds opportunities in every difficulty."[1]

Mandela said, "Part of being optimistic is keeping one's head pointed toward the sun, one's feet moving forward. There were many dark moments when my faith in humanity was sorely tested, but I would not and could not give myself up to despair. That way lay defeat and death."[2]

There were about twenty-five adults from their early twenties to early eighties around the table that year (we're eagerly awaiting grandchildren!), and I asked everyone if they were mostly optimistic or mostly pessimistic. The group split down the middle, with equal numbers in both camps from all age groups.

One baby boomer confessed that though he's primarily a pessimist, his pessimism motivates him to do whatever he can to advance enlightened thinking. This enables him to maintain a measure of idealism and hope in a world that he sees as being on a self-destructive path relative to the environment, technology, and intergroup and international relationships.

Another boomer didn't vote at all because she couldn't identify with either the optimist or the pessimist camp. She's a pragmatic realist, she said, and seeks to creatively and positively manage her life and help others manage theirs in the interests of stimulating greater creativity, productivity, and goodness.

The millennials—there were six or seven of you that year—primarily considered yourselves to be pessimists. You said you were worried about your futures, the job market, and your ability to sustain a lifestyle that you know requires substantial income. You didn't know if you could achieve your goals, be materially satisfied, and maintain passion in your work: You also were wondering what it really means to be successful.

One of you said you feel powerlessness as an individual to substantially change conditions in the world that are so destructive, racist, sexist, tribal, selfish, and self-centered. Yet you are a liberal political activist motivated by deep idealism. Other millennials nodded in agreement as you spoke.

So the question about optimism and pessimism isn't a personal one. It's a communal question for Jews. Who, in essence, are we? Are we optimists or pessimists? Are we hopeful or cynical? Do we feel empowered to fight the good fight or have we given up, resigned ourselves to the world as it is, and decided that it's enough simply to take care of ourselves as best we can and let others do the same? Can we free ourselves and our world from the conditions that most oppress us or are we enslaved by them?

The Case for Optimism—and Activism

Only optimism, I believe, will give us the willingness to expend the time, energy, and resources necessary to free ourselves by fighting injustices, hard-heartedness, cruelty, stupidity, lies, and falsehood that we're fed every day like poisoned wheat. I confess to moments of despair and pessimism, but I'm an optimist, ever gravitating toward being able to appreciate the possibilities of change.

Research supports the view that optimism and the patience that comes with it give people many advantages over those who are pessimistic and impatient. As psychologist and researcher Dr. Timothy Elliott was quoted saying in the *New York Times*, optimists are better at building personal relationships; they're more successful in academics and professional life; they're better at managing love affairs and friendships; and they're more resilient, better able to bear up under stress at work, cope with financial loss, and confront loneliness, illness, and death.[3]

There's a Hebrew expression (though originally from the Islamic Sufi tradition) that embraces the optimistic attitude within Judaism. I repeat this phrase to myself whenever I encounter personal hardship: *Gam zeh ya'avor*, "This too will pass!"

Optimism is clearly better than pessimism; affirmation is better than cynicism. But I'm not going to simply leave you with the studies that say so or with my own opinions. I know you won't feel any differently just because someone says you should. Instead, I want to recommend an experiment. In the face of any pessimism you feel, I hope you'll try something that's always been the classic Jewish antidote to pessimism and cynicism, the Jewish response to disillusionment, and the Jewish hedge against insanity: Get involved in addressing the issues that give you the greatest sense of helplessness and despair. Get active and do something that advances the common good. By being active we become inspired by the urgency of the cause, and this engagement itself overcomes pessimism, cynicism, and despair.

Many of your peers already do this in their lives. I hope they keep it up, dragging their pessimistic and defeated friends in as partners in this struggle. Whenever we sit around our family Shabbat and holiday tables, we ought to be talking about these challenges, arguing about them. After all, that's what we Jews do best. We're masters of nuanced debate. That's the first thing we can do, and we need to do more of it together.

There's no such thing in Judaism as checking out physically and mentally. *Pirkei Avot* reminds us that it's not our duty to finish the task of making our lives and world better, but neither are we free from trying (2:21).

The Talmud records an incident in which Rabbi Yossi bar Hanina, in the years following the destruction of Jerusalem by Rome, was traveling on the road and wanted to pray, so he entered one of the many ruins surrounding Jerusalem. When he completed his prayer, Elijah the Prophet, who'd been watching him, greeted him and asked why he decided to pray amidst ruins.

"Why didn't you pray on the road?" Elijah asked.

Rabbi Yossi answered, "I was afraid of being interrupted by passersby."

Elijah said, "You could have prayed a short prayer" (*B'reishit Rabbah* 24).

What did Elijah mean? Rabbi Yossi shouldn't have wallowed in the destruction that the Jerusalem ruins represented or been immobilized by the pain and negativity, pessimism and cynicism of the tragic Jewish past. And he shouldn't have feared the passersby, expecting them to be dangerous, more powerful and capable than he was. Rather, he should have prayed quickly on the road and kept moving forward, because the road was the pathway to redemption and renewal.

Judaism is about cleaning up the rubble of society. But first we need to recognize that we're in the midst of rubble. Then we get mad about it and emerge from it. We can't wallow in it or be resigned to it and wall ourselves off from it if we're going to *do* something about it.

Rabbi Abraham Joshua Heschel walked with Dr. Martin Luther King Jr. from Selma to Montgomery in a march that helped bring into being the Voting Rights Act of 1965. In what became one of the most beautiful and extraordinary descriptions not only of the civil rights movement but also of the power of love and justice to touch the soul, Rabbi Heschel said that as he marched alongside Dr. King he felt as if "his legs were praying."[4]

Prayer, too, has shown itself to have positive mental, emotional, and physical effects, because effective prayer integrates our minds and hearts, lifts our spirits, gives us hope, fortifies our purpose, and reminds us, as Dr. King preached, that we "are caught in a network of mutuality, tied in a single garment of destiny."[5]

Answering Loss with Lovingkindness

Whenever I've felt despair or a sense of frustration about issues in my life—even when I've sensed I failed myself or someone near and dear to me—the quickest way out of my low feelings has been to do something for someone else. The Jewish category of mitzvah *gemilut hasadim*, deeds of lovingkindness, includes many acts that we do on behalf of others: visit the sick; comfort mourners; show empathy for the brokenhearted; be hospitable; feed the hungry; clothe the poor; work on behalf of the homeless and the ill; celebrate with brides and grooms, people who get promotions in their work and who complete projects about which they feel pride, and on and on. Doing anything on behalf of another human being is a transcendent act. It helps take our minds and hearts off our own worries and concerns.

One of the greatest lessons my mother taught me was how to transcend the pain of loss and loneliness by doing for others. After my father died, she was always the first one to respond to women who lost their husbands in death, who suffered illness, who were lonely. She reached out and, as a single woman for most of her life, she found her salvation in doing so. She often told us that the only thing between her and the world was the front door, and all she had to do was walk through it. And she did, constantly and consistently. She was a superb model of positive activism. She knew intuitively what other people needed because she was fundamentally an empathic woman. She had experienced much loss in her life, and she used the pain that came with it to do kind deeds for others. People loved her for it, and she often received far more from them than she gave. In this way she was an optimist even when she felt despair. She never lost hope.

In his important book *The Anatomy of Hope*, Dr. Jerome Groopman of Harvard Medical School writes:

> Hope differs from optimism. Hope does not arise from being told to "think positively," or from hearing an overly rosy forecast. Hope, unlike optimism, is rooted in unalloyed reality.... Hope is the elevating feeling we experience when we see—in the mind's eye—a path to a better future. Hope acknowledges the significant obstacles and deep pitfalls along that path. True hope has no room for delusion.[6]

Ground Yourself with Hope

I would add one more thought: Hope keeps us grounded in the here and now. A teacher of mine, whose identity is lost to the mists of memory, once inspired me with the characterization of hope as "a commandment of the heart in the face of uncertainty, a vision that opens up the future, based on trust, supportive of purpose, enabling us to live in an enhanced present of constructive waiting."

In other words keeping our focus on the kind of world we want to inhabit, while doing everything possible here and now to prepare ourselves for that future vision and dream, inspires not only hope but also renewed energy and a sense of purpose.

Rabbi Nachman of Breslov said, "Remember: things can go from the very worst to the very best ... in just the blink of an eye."[7]

As a lover of the people and State of Israel, I resonated with what my good friend Yaron Shavit, former chair of the Israel Movement for Progressive Judaism and a commander in the Israeli reserves, once said to me: *b'Yisrael ye-ush lo optsia,* "In Israel, despair is not an option." I would expand Yaron's statement and say *b'chayim, ye-ush lo optsia,* in life, despair is not an option!

Each of us has the ability to make tremendous changes with the smallest of actions. Remember what started with Rosa Parks refusing to give up her rightful seat and how individual voices demanding marriage equality did the impossible and changed society and the law. And take inspiration from our own history, the story of Nachshon, the son of Aminadav, who plays a significant role in the story of the Exodus, though he's little known in the Haggadah.

Nachshon isn't mentioned in the biblical Exodus story per se, yet he looms large in rabbinic literature as a critically important figure in the narrative at the Sea of Reeds.[8] It's written that as the Israelites fled Egypt, they were trapped between the impassable sea ahead and the Egyptian army that pursued them. Terrified, they turned on Moses and cried, "Why did you bring us here to perish?"

> Rabbi Judah says: "When the Israelites stood at the sea, one said, 'I don't want to go down to the sea first.' Another said, 'I don't want to go down first either.' While they were standing there, and while Moses was praying to God to save them, Nachshon the son of Aminadav jumped up, went down, and fell into the waves."[9]

What's the meaning of this midrash?

First, it seems to me that that Moses's prayers were insufficient to convince God to split the sea. Only when Nachshon took the initiative and jumped into the waters did God respond.

Second, at a very early stage in Israel's history there was a basic understanding about the mutual relationship between God and humankind. Though the people might have felt alone and abandoned, God was with them all along.

Nachshon's "leap" was a significant turning point in the Jewish experience. His willingness to take history into his own hands became a tenet of Jewish religious activism and a defining element in the character of the Jewish hero.

My childhood rabbi and good friend Rabbi Richard Levy has written concerning *karpas*, one of the symbolic foods that appears on the traditional Seder plate—the greens that represent spring, dipped in the salt water that represents the tears of slavery:

> On the nights of Passover we celebrate Israel crossing the ... sea from slavery to freedom. In this light, *karpas* has other overtones: We remember the heroic example of Nachshon ben Aminadav, who was the first to step into the salty sea. As the Israelites faced the raging waters, Nachshon alone plunged in. Because of his courage, the

Midrash tells us, God divided the sea in two so that all the people of Israel could walk across. When our *karpas* represents Nachshon … the salt water no longer suggests tears, but the grit of heroes.[10]

Jewish activism is founded upon optimism and hope. It can transform even the most despairing among us. Never despair, my sons; never despair!

Love,
Dad

Forgiveness

Dear Daniel and David:

Far too often when I'm called to officiate at a funeral and meet with the family of the deceased, someone is missing from the inner circle of close relatives and friends—a brother, sister, child, or longtime friend. They're absent not because they're unavailable but because some serious breach occurred long before and the parties never forgave one another or reconciled.

Forgiving those who have wronged us is one of the most difficult things we ever do and one of the most important things we ought to do for our own well-being. In the heat of the moment, it can feel impossible, I know. So I'd like to share one of the most remarkable and admittedly most extreme stories of forgiveness I've ever heard, to show you that we humans are capable of doing things we may never have thought possible—even forgiving the "unforgivable."

Imagine this true story related by Rabbi Jack Kornfield:

> One fourteen-year-old boy … shot and killed an innocent teenager to prove himself to his gang. At the trial, the victim's mother sat silently impassive, until the end, when the youth was convicted of the killing. After the verdict was announced, she stood up slowly and stared directly at him and stated, "I'm going to kill you." Then the youth was taken away to serve several years in the juvenile facility.
>
> After the first half year the mother of the slain child went to visit his killer. He had been living on the streets before the killing, and she was the only visitor he had. For a time they talked, and when she left she gave him some money for cigarettes. Then she started step by step

to visit him more regularly, bringing food and small gifts. Near the end of his three-year sentence she asked him what he would be doing when he got out. He was confused and very uncertain, so she offered to set him up with a job at a friend's company. Then she inquired about where he would live, and since he had no family to return to, she offered him temporary use of the spare room in her home.

For eight months he lived there, ate her food, and worked at the job. Then one evening she called him into the living room to talk....

"Do you remember in the courtroom when I said I was going to kill you?"

"I sure do," he replied.

"Well, I did," she went on. "I did not want the boy who could kill my son for no reason to remain alive on this earth. I wanted him to die. That's why I started to visit you and bring you things. That's why I got you the job and let you live here in my house. That's how I set about changing you. And that old boy, he's gone. So now I want to ask you, since my son is gone, and that killer is gone, if you'll stay here. I've got room, and I'd like to adopt you if you let me." And she became the mother of her son's killer, the mother he never had.[1]

Could you have done what that woman did—see into the boy's heart and recognize his potential for transformation? Could you have felt such enormous rage and grief and have been capable of such transcendence?

Honestly, I don't think I could have. We know people, dear friends, whose loved ones were murdered, and I feel nothing but anger toward their killers. I have written letters to the parole board urging them never to release that man, who murdered his wife in front of their small children, not only because he nearly destroyed a family and isn't repentant but also because I could never forgive him for what he did if it had happened to someone in my family.

Yet seemingly impossible forgiveness isn't an anomaly. The story of the woman who adopted her son's killer is remarkable and similar to an account in a book called *Revenge: A Story of Hope* by Laura Blumenfeld. Laura's American father was shot in the head by a Palestinian terrorist in 1986, just steps away from the Kotel (the Western Wall, the holiest site in Judaism) in the Old City of Jerusalem. He survived, but only because the shooter had bad aim. Laura, a journalist with the *Washington Post*, was haunted by her need for revenge, a desire to restore some cosmic balance to her world by exacting justice on the shooter and his family. And so a decade later she went looking for him.

Laura found his family, told them she was researching a story on families caught up in world conflicts, and over time established a relationship with them. She also gained access to the shooter in his Israeli prison cell. She never told him or his family who she really was or revealed that her father was the person left for dead on the cold stone street.

Over time she got to know them, and they grew to trust and love her. To her dismay she grew close to them as well. Laura experienced much on this journey: hate, resentment, disgust, and then empathy and compassion. She discovered over time that the shooter came to regret his act, not because he was wasting away in prison but rather because he realized that what he did was morally wrong and that the person he shot was innocent and undeserving of what was done to him.

Eventually the man came up for parole, and Laura went to the court for the hearing. After his lawyer had spoken and before the judge ruled, she insisted on being heard. The man's family was stunned that she would so presumptuously intrude. The judge refused to let her speak at first because he thought she was a third party with no direct interest in the case. Then she told the court that she had a right to speak because the man this shooter tried to kill was her father.

The courtroom fell silent, and the Arab family was aghast. The judge granted her time. In fact, Laura's mother was in the courtroom as well, and shouted out from the back of the room that if she could forgive this man, then certainly the State of Israel could as well.[2] (However, the State of Israel disagreed, and, as far as I know, the shooter remains in prison).

Could any of us imagine being Laura Blumenfeld, who began with the need for revenge and found her way to forgiveness?

When I think about the journeys of the bereaved mother and the enraged journalist, I'm forced to remind myself that they're real, not fictional, and reflect on what we human beings are really made of, and how vast are our capacities both to hate and ultimately to forgive.

All of us will be hurt, sometimes deeply. Knowing that, our task is to determine how we'll cope when we or one of our dear ones are victimized, and what we'll have to do to arrive at a place of forgiveness.

Six Truths about Forgiveness

As I've thought about how to forgive, how to reach the place inside that allows us to lay down the burdens that come with being wronged, I've gleaned six truths about the nature of forgiveness:

1. Forgiveness is a step-by-step process and not a single event.

Forgiveness involves a gradual peeling away, layer by layer, of accumulated hurt, rage, resentment, grief, regret, and revenge, with the ultimate goal of reopening the heart to compassion, love, wisdom, and harmony. True forgiveness doesn't paper over what happened to us, nor does it suppress or ignore our pain. It can't be hurried. It comes only when we're able to honor the grief and sense of betrayal that are part of us and part of our past without letting them take over our lives in the present.

2. Forgiveness requires a courageous act of will.

Forgiveness is not about forgetting, pardoning, condoning, falsely reconciling, or appeasing an aggressor or wrongdoer. As Eknath Easwaran summarizes the great Hindu scripture the Bhagavad Gita, "If you want to see the brave, look at those who can forgive. If you want to see the heroic, look at those who can love in return for hatred."[3]

Forgiving takes fortitude, which is why Mahatma Gandhi teaches that "The weak can never forgive. Forgiveness is the attribute of the strong."[4]

3. Forgiveness requires us to believe in our basic goodness.

Forgiveness needs to be anchored in the belief that we're nobly born by virtue of being created *b'tzelem Elohim*, in the divine image, and that we have an innate capacity for wisdom, purity, goodness, and love. Our noble birth doesn't mean of course that we're always loving, good, pure, and wise, or that we always behave morally and well. But it does mean that we aspire to do better, even when we are hurt and justifiably filled with the desire to seek vengeance.

4. Forgiveness frees us.

When we hold on to our anger and resentment, we bind ourselves to the person who hurt us, creating an emotional link that's stronger than steel.

The only means to dissolve that link is through forgiveness—that is, letting go. Forgiveness is therefore a conscious act of will and choice.

Viktor Frankl writes, "Between a stimulus and response there is a space. In that space is our power to choose our response. In our response lies our growth and our freedom. The last of human freedoms is to choose one's attitude in any given set of circumstances."[5]

If we say of someone who hurt us, "I'll never forgive that person," we consign ourselves to a prison in which we're both the jailor and the prisoner. Consider this dialogue between two former prisoners of war:

"Have you forgiven your captors yet?"

"No! Never!"

"Well, then, they still have you in prison, don't they?"[6]

When asked if he could ever forgive the Chinese for their military occupation of Tibet and the systematic destruction of Tibetan monasteries and culture, the Dalai Lama is said to have replied, "They've already taken my country. Why should I let them have my mind, too?"[7]

Forgiveness doesn't depend on anyone except us—it's unilateral. It doesn't require the other person to apologize or ask to be forgiven. It doesn't even require the other person to be alive or aware of our decision to forgive. As difficult as it is to do, forgiveness is ultimately very simple—it means releasing ourselves from the pain inflicted upon us in the past and letting it go in the present. This we can do by ourselves, for ourselves, with the support of our family and friends.

5. Forgiveness means acknowledging our pain.

Before we can forgive others, we have to feel fully the injury we have sustained, grieve as if we have suffered the death of a loved one, and then reconstitute our lives after an appropriate period of mourning. This is perhaps the most difficult challenge of all, because so many of us have allowed our hurt, grief, fear, resentment, and rage to pile up over time, one negative emotion sitting on top of another, each adding density to our negative feelings. We have created a veritable black hole of intensifying negativity that sucks the life out of everyone around us.

Many people wrongly assume we should simply move on, without needing to do emotional work. Negative emotions don't go anywhere. They stay inside us, buried, and they'll rear their heads when we least expect it. To make forgiveness possible, we need to strive to understand how a hurt fits into the rest of our lives, how it's changed us and our world view, and how it has closed our hearts.

The goal of forgiveness is a reshaped life, and if we come to it late, forgiveness can reshape death as well. We'll know that the process of forgiveness has been effective and that we're different when we can recall those who have hurt us and nevertheless want to wish them well.

6. "Forgiveness ... doesn't rewrite history, but it does allow us to rewrite our *story* of our history."[8]

Our willingness to change and then to see the world through a more positive lens resets the compass of the heart so we can reclaim our larger self, our larger consciousness, our larger capacity for lovingkindness. It allows us to open our hearts to others, and it frees us from the debilitating fear of being hurt again.

Fear, anger, and rage turn us in upon ourselves if we don't attend to them. Forgiveness opens us outward to others. Fear and anger keep us stuck in the past. Forgiveness opens us to the present. Anger rails at what happened yesterday. Forgiveness means giving up all hope that yesterday will be better than it was.

Forgiveness requires us to be honest with ourselves about what has happened to us and to see past hurt in the larger context of who we have become. As we do this, forgiveness puts us back on track toward restoring our integrity and dignity.

A story is told of a righteous baker. Though he was a man of many virtues, the people of his village kept their distance from him, fearing his righteous fury. They preferred to keep company with his wife, who respected her husband and loved him, but even she ached for something more than his righteousness.

One morning, having worked since before dawn to knead dough for his ovens, the baker came home and, to his shock, found his wife in bed with a stranger. The woman's adultery soon became the talk of the town, and everyone assumed that the baker would throw his wife out of the house. But he kept her as his wife, saying that he forgave her as the Good Book said he should—that's how a virtuous man should live.

In his heart of hearts, though, he could never forgive his wife for bringing shame upon him and his good name. In his mind he had only anger for her, and he hated her for betraying him.

The baker's duplicity was recognized in heaven. Each time he felt hatred for his wife, an angel came to him and dropped a small pebble the size of a shirt button into his heart. And each time a pebble dropped, he felt a stab of pain, just like the pain he felt that day when he discovered his wife and another man in their bed.

He hated her, and his hate brought him more pain, and his pain made him hate even more deeply than before. The pebbles multiplied, and the baker's heart grew so heavy with their weight that the top half of his body bent forward and he had to strain his neck upward to see straight ahead. Weary with hurt, he wished he were dead.

One night the angel with the pebbles told the baker he could be healed of his hurt. The remedy was the "miracle of the magic eyes." He'd need eyes that could look back to the beginning of his pain and see his wife not as a woman who betrayed him but as a weak woman who needed him. Only a new way of looking at things through these magic eyes could heal the hurt flowing from yesterday's wounds.

The baker protested. "Nothing can change the past," he said. "She's guilty, and not even an angel from heaven can change that."

The angel responded, "You're right. You can't change the past. You can only heal the wounds that come to you from the past. And you can only heal them with the vision of the magic eyes."

The baker asked how he could get the magic eyes. "Just ask," said the angel, "and they'll be given to you. And each time you see your wife through the new eyes, one pebble will be lifted from your aching heart."

It took the baker some time to ask for the magic eyes because he'd grown to love his hatred. But his pain finally drove him to make the request, and the angel delivered. Soon he was living with a different woman, a woman in need who actually loved him rather than a wicked woman who had betrayed him. He had the same wife, of course, but she was transformed by his new eyes.

The angel kept his promise. One by one the pebbles were lifted from the baker's heart, though it took a long time to take them all away. Gradually the baker's heart grew lighter, and he began to stand straight again.

He invited his wife back into his heart, and together they set out on a new journey, building upon the past but not bound to it.

When we forgive, this story teaches, we heal hurts we don't deserve inflicted unfairly and callously by others. The choice is ours. We can hold on to our injuries, or we can begin the work of forgiving, not for the sake of the other but for our own sake. By forgiving we reverse the flow of our own history. We're released from the pain that was born in the past but has poisoned our present.

The theologian Lewis Smedes writes, "When we forgive, we come as close as any human being can to the essentially divine act of creation. For we create a new beginning out of past pain that never had a right to exist in the first place.... When we forgive, we heal the hurt we never deserved."[9]

There's a traditional Jewish prayer said at bedtime each night:

> Creator of the universe, I hereby forgive anyone who angered or antagonized me or who sinned against me—whether against my body, my property, my honor, or anything of mine; whether done accidentally, willfully, carelessly, or purposely; whether through speech, deed, thought, or notion; whether in this transmigration or another transmigration—I forgive every Jew and every person.
>
> May no person be punished because of me. May it be Your will, Adonai, my God and the God of my ancestors, that I may sin no more. Whatever transgressions I have done before You, may You blot out in Your abundant mercies, but not through suffering or bad illness.
>
> May the words of my mouth and the meditations of my heart be acceptable before You, Adonai, my Rock and my Redeemer. Amen.

To forgive is to live free of the encumbrances of the past. All that's required is simply to decide to let go. When we do, life becomes a great adventure.

Love,
Dad

A Blessing

Dear Daniel and David:

I've shared much of my thinking, along with my values, passions, concerns, and life experiences, with you in these letters. I hope they speak to the questions with which you struggle and that they become touchstones for you. I hope as well that you'll let your disagreements and unique insights become starting points for discussion and debate with me, in our family, and among your friends.

Now I'd like to leave you with a blessing, in much the same way I did when you were young and we sat as a family around our Shabbat table, lighting candles, singing *kiddush* and *hamotzi*. Each week I blessed you, though you didn't always want me to do it. I hope that you'll accept the blessing I offer you now and that when you have children of your own, you'll share it with them, *l'dor vador*, from generation to generation.

I offer you this more expansive blessing not only because I love you so dearly but also because I want you to know that after Mom and I married each other, the greatest joy and fulfillment we have known has been your coming into the world. You have been precious gifts to us, and I'm grateful beyond words.

Here is my blessing for you—and for every adult child in our community:

> May you remember always that life is a gift,
> that good health is a blessing,

and that family love is irreplaceable.

May you enjoy fulfilment in love and in work,
and may you discover what's possible in a marriage worthy of God's
    blessing.

May the fruits of your love—your children—add value to the world,
and may you each be inspired to create your life as a work of art.

May you each continue to grow wise in heart
as you live your life fully and well.
May songs of gratitude pass your lips
as you exult in the created world.
And may you be open always to wonder and amazement.

May you each expand the reach of your soul
through simple acts of lovingkindness,
in giving of yourself to others,
and through good and righteous deeds.

May your soul be enriched
through quiet meditation and prayer
and in your engagement with the Jewish community, Jewish people, and
    State of Israel.
May your study of Judaism inspire you,
and may you become one with the rhythms of Jewish living
and be more than you ever imagined you could be.

May the words of our prophets and sages light up your life,
and our people's accomplishments in Israel and the lands of the Diaspora
fill you with pride and joy in being a Jew.

May your family and friends comfort you in painful times.

May optimism and faith sustain you and give you courage.

May your hopes and dreams be fulfilled.

May you be blessed with patience and understanding,
humility, awe, and wonder,
and may you pursue all things that are good.

Your mother and I love you.

As brothers, may you love each other always,

supporting and sustaining each other in good times and bad.

Finally, I offer you the blessing you heard so often at our family Shabbat table:

Y'sim'chem Elohim k'Ephraim u'k'Manasseh—

May you be like Ephraim and Manasseh,

who carried forward the life of our people.

[for your daughters, should you have them]

Y'sim'chen Elohim k'Sarah, Rivkah, Rachel v'Leah—

May you be like Sarah, Rebecca, Rachel, and Leah,

who carried forward the life of our people.

[For a boy]

Y'varech'cha Adonai v'yishm'recha.

Ya'er Adonai panav eilecha vichuneka.

Yisa Adonai panav eilecha v'yasem l'cha shalom.

[The same blessing, for a girl]

Y'va-rech Adonai v'yishm'rech.

Ya'er Adonai panav eilayich vi'chunech.

Yisa Adonai panav eilayich v'yasem lach shalom.

May God bless you and keep you.

May God's light shine upon you and be gracious to you.

May God's light be lifted upon you and grant you peace.

I love you—I love you—I love you!

Amen.

Afterword

Daniel and David Rosove

Author's note: I asked my sons, Daniel and David, to offer an afterword for this series of letters, and what follows is what they have written.

Daniel has worked for years in two NGOs—J Street in Washington, DC, and Los Angeles; and Mazon: A Jewish Response to Hunger in Los Angeles. David has been working in the entertainment industry, including in talent agencies, at CBS in prime-time programming, and as a digital producer of short subjects intended for the millennial generation at TNT in Los Angeles.

They wrote their thoughts in the style of a Google chat, which is how they often communicate with each other and with their friends.

DavidRosove *signs on to Google Hangouts*

DanielRosove *signs on to Google Hangouts*

Daniel: Hey David, did you finish Dad's book?

David: Hey Daniel, yeah, I just did.

Daniel: So what did you think of it?

David: I loved reading it. Had you ever heard of an ethical will? I had never given my own legacy much thought. I have trouble imagining what my future life will be like, especially since I'm still so young, and it's hard for me to think about how I want to be remembered. But what struck me is the idea that every action we take now contributes to the legacy we leave behind. Dad's writing that at this stage of his life carried a lot of weight for me. What'd you think?

Daniel: I agree. I was just beaming.

The letter about how to judge a good life moved me. He believes even small actions can grow into so much more. It's the greatest lesson he has taught me, that what we do and say matters, that life is about making the world and the lives of those around us better.

I hadn't thought of the ethical will either. I love it! You think you'd write one? What would it say?

David: I think I will. There are a few categories that come to mind immediately. Will I have raised good, upstanding children? Will they respect others and treat people with kindness? I'm professionally driven so I wonder, will making a lot of money actually satisfy me? Or should the goal only be happiness in whatever job I have? It's probably some combination of both, but I want people to remember that I worked hard, was honest, and made decisions that I was proud of. What about you? What's the first thing that comes to mind?

Daniel: This is difficult. At this point in my life I still have so many questions. How can we possibly know what our futures will hold?

David: It seems daunting, doesn't it?

Daniel: Totally. I would start by urging my kids to value family and community, to look upon our people's traditions with deep pride, and to be motivated, excited, and inspired to pass those traditions on to the next generation. They should know the importance of being honest with others and with themselves. To listen to their innermost trusted voice and try to live a life that has meaning and improves the lives of others. They need to know that shaking their fists at the world's problems isn't good enough. We must take that energy and turn it into action.

> **David:** I find it interesting that when we start talking about how we want to be remembered, we immediately think of the children we're going to have. This is our first thought. Why is that? For me, I see myself as an extension of our parents. More and more, I find myself saying and doing things that feel so much like Mom and Dad; it's scary. So it does make sense that I'd want the same for my kids. I think you and I have had a pretty great example in them of a loving marriage, and they have certainly done a great job raising us. I want my kids to feel the same about me. But times are different; the world has changed. How do we replicate what Mom and Dad have done for us? I think this begs the question, as part of the millennial generation, what is inherently different about us? How has growing up in the twenty-first century changed the way we think about our lives, our family, and our Judaism?

Daniel: One thing that is certainly changing is how Jews meet, who we marry, and how we engage our community.

> **David:** Absolutely. I think you and I might have different perspectives on this—in particular on intermarriage. I don't know if I've ever told Dad this, but his decision to officiate at intermarriages had a major impact on me. I had long struggled with the idea that I could fall in love with a person who isn't Jewish and that our father would not be able to officiate at the wedding ceremony. It tore at me. It even affected some of my past relationships. But when he gave that sermon to rousing applause from the congregation, it gave me chills. It told me that he understood how people's lives are so different nowadays. I don't know who I am going to marry. I don't know if she will be Jewish or not. But what I do know is that I have the freedom to choose whomever I want and Dad will be there right underneath the chuppah with me. It makes me so happy.

Daniel: I think about this differently. I'm a bit more traditional. My identity is very much tied to our tribal past and present. To me, marrying a woman who was raised Jewish matters. I'm upset that our generation has an intermarriage rate of 60 to 70 percent. However, what is most important is raising Jewish children—to uphold, as Dad said in his letter to us, "Jewish continuity."

I mean, that's why I suffered through two years of online Jewish dating in Los Angeles, haha! If the woman really wanted to convert, I would have been OK with that.

> **David:** Oy. Maybe Temple Israel should have a Tinder night. Yikes … even typing those words makes the hair on my back stand up.
>
> I do want to point out, however, that even though there's a possibility that I won't marry a Jew, I definitely, 100 percent, without a doubt, want to raise my kids as Jews and have a Jewish household. Not only because Jewish life and culture are so ingrained in me, but also because it's important to me (and I think to you and Dad) that our kids truly understand Seinfeld humor! Actually, that might be the most important thing about parenting in general. Look to the cookie!
>
> Anyway, Daniel, we both agree that we want to raise Jewish families, but how we get there is a little different. What about belief in God?

Daniel: I became a believer in God when I went to Israel and touched the Western Wall when I was thirteen, and I lost that belief when I went to Israel again when I was nineteen. Seeing what the modern Jewish people had created inspired my faith in the human spirit. It didn't make me want to thank God. When I returned to the U.S., Dad and I engaged for months on the topic. He went out and bought me many books by Rabbi Abraham Joshua Heschel.

Truth is, at the time I was too young, combative, and literal-minded to understand what Dad was trying to tell me, that the sense of *awe*, as elucidated by Heschel, is the source of his faith in God and in the wonder and unity in the universe. Now, if I were to let myself say the words "I believe in God," I would see it through Dad's eyes. The sense of awe I get at beautiful scenery, the love I have for my girlfriend or playing drums, the connection I have with family and my closest friends. In the spaces in between those feelings, I can find something divine.

David: So where else do you feel the sense of awe?

Daniel: When I connect with an animal, see a sunset, think about the infinite enormity and smallness of the universe, many times, my mind just stops comprehending what I'm experiencing. Perhaps that is where I can find holiness. Did what Dad say in his letter to us speak to you?

David: The title of the letter "You Don't Have to Believe in God to Be a Jew" might sum up my entire experience as a Jew, and especially as a millennial Jew. I sometimes consider myself to be more culturally Jewish than religiously Jewish. I don't believe in God as an almighty force, but I do believe in a shared sense of community and togetherness. I feel this the most when I'm in Israel. The moment I step off the plane (even after I feel complete embarrassment when people clap their hands upon landing), I feel different. It's the sense that I'm a part of something much greater than myself, that I can look into a stranger's eyes and have a deep understanding of who they are just because we both share the same religion and are part of the same people. I think there is a certain kind of awe that comes from that indescribable connection we Jews feel with one another. Maybe this is what God is to me. I think my relationship to God is deeply tied to feeling Jewish, and therefore to Israel.

Daniel: I really agree. If I were to go to the core of my Jewish identity, it would be based on my ever-evolving relationship with Zionism and Israel.

Millennials have had a different experience of Israel than our parents and grandparents. Our grandparents witnessed Israel's birth. Baby boomers saw Israel retake Jerusalem and become a regional power.

For us and our fellow millennials, our formative experience regarding Israel was the Second Intifada and the lack of a resolution of the conflict with the Palestinians. We love Israel but we also love universal human rights.

I am an aspirational Zionist. So my Judaism, as Dad so eloquently said, at its root level holds that "we are tied to the destiny and fate of the State of Israel wherever we live." I still get chills that I am alive at this moment in Jewish history when the State of Israel is a reality. We are so lucky. It hadn't happened for almost two thousand years! I just want our generation to engage with Israel in a different way than our parents and grandparents do.

> David: It is weird to think about a world and many generations before us who have had such a different experience of Israel than you and I have. To be honest I think I do take it for granted, and I think it's easy to do so. We both grew up knowing that our father lived in Israel during the Yom Kippur War. We traveled there as a family when I was only eight years old, then again when I was eighteen, and then I went once more for my Birthright trip at twenty-two. Israel has been steadfast throughout my entire life, and it's hard to imagine a world where Israel doesn't exist. In fact I don't want to imagine that world. I'm not sure where my complacency on the State of Israel comes from, especially considering that I have you as a brother and Dad as a father. But I've never seriously thought about losing Israel. Are you optimistic about its future?

Daniel: I am at my core a Zionist. To be a Zionist means I am driven by deeply optimistic ideals about how Israel should and could be. But I am not the first or the last to say that Israel is at an existential crossroads. One road takes Israel down a path of pessimism and away from optimism. Is Israel going to turn toward intolerance, hypernationalism, and religious bigotry, or

will it correct itself, going back to its optimism and the ideals expressed in its Declaration of Independence? That is the
key question. So I am an optimist because we can't afford not
to care about Israel, its people, and its future. But there is no
guarantee of success.

I suppose I am no longer that millennial around our Passover
table that Dad alluded to, the one who is upset and fearful of
the destructive, racist, sexist, tribal, selfish, and self-centered
forces in the world. They are still there—they could even have
the upper hand in some cases—but I deeply believe that any
humanmade problem can be unmade by human action. That is
my optimism at work.

I once heard someone say that cynics are optimists who are
in search of something to believe in but aren't able to find it. I
work to find my causes. I fight for them and am optimistic that
we can one day win.

> **David:** I was one of those six or seven people at our Passover
> Seder who raised his hand as a pessimist. I think that is rel-
> atively common among my friends and age group. It's hard
> to be all bright and shiny about the future of not only our
> country but of Israel as well. But my pessimism, as I've dis-
> covered through reading Dad's book, is more about the self-
> ish, personal, and materialistic facets of my life. Am I going
> to make enough money to support the lifestyle I want to live?
> Is that even possible? Are my kids going to be lucky enough
> to go to good schools? Am I going to find happiness in what-
> ever I choose to do professionally? These are the ethical will
> questions we just mentioned. I don't know. Maybe this is just
> uncertainty.
>
> On the other hand, I am optimistic about certain things that
> are on a much grander scale. I am optimistic that there always
> will be a State of Israel. I am optimistic that somehow, some
> way, our country will improve economically and become more
> socially tolerant and just. So I guess my life isn't completely

devoid of optimism. Am I a pessimistic optimist? Is that even a thing? I can feel optimism because I know there are people out there, like you and Dad, who are fighting the good fight and who seem to have an overwhelming sense of hope that I can't help but feel too.

Daniel: I really appreciate that, but I think I learned that from Dad.

David: Don't forget about Mom.

Daniel: He wouldn't be who he is without her. Remember, she read every High Holy Day sermon he ever wrote and gave him her honest feedback.

David: Oh right, that's true. Come to think of it, we should probably send this to Mom before he sees it. If that's worked for him all these years, why wouldn't it work for us?

Daniel: Sounds good; send it. I have a meeting to get to. I'll talk to you later.

David: All right. Talk soon.

DavidRosove signs out of Google Hangouts

DanielRosove signs out of Google Hangouts

Acknowledgments

This book could not have been completed without my first editor, Donna Frazier Glynn, whose gentle hand, response with the material, and keen understanding of the audience for whom I intended these letters helped shape and tune this volume. I am also grateful to Emily Wichland at Turner Publishing, who helped bring the manuscript to the end result.

I'm grateful to many people who read early drafts, including Rabbi Ammi Hirsch of the Stephen Wise Free Synagogue in New York City; Letty Cottin Pogrebin, writer, Zionist, feminist, and peace activist; Susan Core Freudenheim, former executive editor of the *Los Angeles Jewish Journal* and now the director of Jewish World Watch; and Rabbi John Moscowitz, who urged me to write a book after reading my blogs.

I'm grateful to my colleagues, friends, and congregants at Temple Israel of Hollywood who have taught me much over the nearly three decades I have served this special community, and to my first rabbinic mentor, Rabbi Martin S. Weiner, who set me on a solid and meaningful path in the rabbinate, and who, along with his wife Karen, remain both Barbara's and my dear friends after all these years.

Most of all, I'm grateful to my wife, Barbara, who has been my partner in all things and my dearest and most cherished friend; to my sons, Daniel and David, for whom I wrote these letters; and to my brother, Dr. Michael Rosove, whose support of me in so many ways has been a constant throughout my life.

Notes

You Don't Have to Believe in God to Be a Jew

1. Carl Sagan, *Pale Blue Dot: A Vision of the Human Future in Space* (New York: Random House, 1994), 152–53.

2. Abraham Joshua Heschel, *Between God and Man: An Interpretation of Judaism* (London: Collier Macmillan, 1959), 47.

3. Rabbi Menachem Mendel of Vitebsk (1730–1788) was an early third-generational leader of Hasidic Judaism and was the primary disciple of the Maggid of Mezeritch. He lived in Minsk and served his hasidim in Belarus.

Why Religion Still Has Value

1. Jonathan Sacks, *The Dignity of Difference: How to Avoid the Clash of Civilizations* (London: Bloomsbury, 2002), 53.

2. According to the science of gematria, the ancient Assyro-Babylonian system of numerology that assigns number equivalents to the letters of the Hebrew aleph-bet (e.g., *aleph* = 1; *bet* = 2; *gimmel* = 3; *daled* = 4), the total number equivalent in each verse (Leviticus 19:18 and Deuteronomy 6:5) is the same: 907. There is also a mystical numerological connection that can be made between the Hebrew words *ahavah* (love), *echad* (one), and YHVH:

     Ahavah (aleph/1 + heh/5 + vav/6 + heh/1) = 13

     Echad (aleph /1 + chet/8 + daled/4) = 13

     Echad + Echad = 26

     Ahavah + Ahavah = 26

     YHVH (yod/10 + heh/5 + vav/6 + heh/5) = 26

3. I learned this concept of *Zwischeninstanz* ("in-betweenness") as a rabbinic student at the Hebrew Union College in Los Angeles when I studied Martin Buber's "I-Thou" philosophy of relationship. Buber affirmed that in every I-Thou relationship there is a third Thou that is revealed "in between" (*Zwischeninstanz*) that he characterized as the "Eternal Thou" (i.e., God). As

a non-German speaker, I asked Ruth Nussbaum, the widow of Rabbi Max
Nussbaum, who had served Rabbi Leo Baeck as one of his assistant rabbis in
Berlin between 1936 and 1940 and was my predecessor as the senior rabbi
of Temple Israel of Hollywood (1942–1974), how she understood the Ger-
man *Zwischeninstanz* ("inbetweenness"). She confirmed to me Martin Buber's
German notion of the "Eternal Thou" presenting Itself—*Zwischeninstanz*.

4. Jonathan Sacks, *Not in God's Name: Confronting Religious Violence* (New York:
Schocken Books, 2015), 54.

5. Ibid., 76.

6. Ibid., 179.

7. See Martin Buber, *Tales of the Chassidim* (New York: Schocken Books,
1947), 77.

8. Amy Eilberg, *From Enemy to Friend: Jewish Wisdom and the Pursuit of Peace*
(New York: Orbis, 2014), 75–76.

Why I Support Couples Who Intermarry (and Agreed to Officiate at Their Weddings)

1. Joseph Soloveitchik, "Mt. Sinai—Their Finest Hour," in *Reflections of the
Rav: Lessons in Jewish Thought*, vol. 1, ed. Abraham R. Besdin (Hoboken, NJ:
KTAV, 1993), 91.

2. Pew Research Center, "A Portrait of Jewish Americans," October 1, 2013,
www.pewforum.org/2013/10/01/jewish-american-beliefs-attitudes-culture-survey.
For Dr. Cohen's discussion of the implications of
this survey, see http://huc.edu/news/article/2013/
survey-researcher-dr-steven-m-cohen-implications-pew-study.

3. Ibid.

4. My gratitude extends to my classmate and colleague Rabbi Janet Marder of
Temple Beth Am, Los Altos Hills, who led the way by offering such a blessing during the High Holy Days in her community.

5. As I indicated in the sermon itself, I struggled with the issue of rabbinic officiating of intermarriage throughout my career, since being ordained rabbi
at HUC-JIR in New York in 1979. My decision to change my policy came
following years of intense conversation with many people. In particular, I
am indebted to my friends and colleagues who helped me reconsider my
position. They include Letty Cottin Pogrebin and her husband, Bert Pogrebin; Lynn Povich and her husband, Stephen Shepherd; my cousins Susan
Bay-Nimoy and Leonard Nimoy; Rabbi Lawrence A. Hoffman, my teacher
and friend of close to forty years; and my colleague Rabbi Peter Rubinstein.

Though I do not know Michael J. Fox personally, I was moved by his
description of his experience with his wife, Tracy Pollan, as their son,
Sam, prepared to become bar mitzvah at Rabbi Rubinstein's synagogue,
Central Synagogue in New York City (see *Always Looking Up: A Memoir* by

Michael J. Fox). I was especially touched by Michael's reaction to a High Holy Day sermon Peter delivered on this issue a number of years ago. Learning of Michael's experience and then having a long talk with Larry Hoffman were what persuaded me that the time had come to change my position.

I am grateful as well for the support of three of my synagogue's past presidents: Keri Hausner, Bill Simon, and Steven Sloan. Most of all, I thank my wife, Barbara, who was the first to challenge me to reconsider my position many years ago. Last but certainly not least are the myriad congregants who responded so positively to my change of policy. I know that there are some in my community who do not agree with my decision, but as I respect them I hope they respect me and the reasons I chose to do as I have done.

6. Soloveitchik, *Reflections of the Rav*, 91–92.

Creating a Jewish Home

1. *The Empty Chair—Finding Hope and Joy: Timeless Wisdom from a Hasidic Master, Rebbe Nachman of Breslov*, adapted by Moshe Mykoff and the Breslov Research Institute from *Rabbi Nachman's Wisdom* (Woodstock, VT: Jewish Lights, 1994), 50.

2. Elie Wiesel, *The Jews of Silence* (New York: Signet, 1967), 79.

3. Abraham Joshua Heschel, *Man's Quest for God* (New York: Scribner, 1954), 44. Heschel sites Seah Sarfe Kodesh, vol. 2, p. 92 for the original.

4. Milton Steinberg, *Basic Judaism* (New York: Harvest, 1947), 129–30.

5. Naomi Levy, *To Begin Again* (New York: Alfred A. Knopf, 1998), 209–10.

6. "Religious Attendance Linked to Lower Mortality in Elderly," July 22, 1999, DukeHealth, https://corporate.dukehealth.org/news-listing/religious-attendance-linked-lower-mortality-elderly.

Embracing Shades of Gray and Finding Peace in the World and at Home

1. Aviezer Ravitzky. "Peace," *20th Century Jewish Religious Thought*. Edited by Arthur A. Cohen and Paul Mendes-Flohr. (Jewish Publication Society: Philadelphia, 2009), 685

2. The *Midrash Rabbah* is the complete collection of Rabbinic sermons based on biblical texts compiled after the end of the first millennium CE. The *Zohar* is a mystical commentary on the Torah written in Spain circa the thirteenth century.

Why Your Generation Should Care about Israel's Future

1. Shabtai Shavit, "For the First Time, I Fear for the Future of Zionism," *Haaretz*, November 24, 2014, www.haaretz.com/opinion/. premium-1.628038.

2. David Ben-Gurion, *Netzach Yisrael* [Eternity of Israel] (Tel Aviv: Aynot Publishing, 1964), 226, my translation. I am grateful to former United States

ambassador to Egypt and Israel Daniel Kurtzer of Princeton University and a biographer of David Ben-Gurion who referred me to Leanna Feldman, director of the Ben-Gurion Archives at Ben-Gurion University of the Negev. Leanna provided me a photocopy of the Hebrew text in which Ben-Gurion's statement appears. To the best of my knowledge, this is the only citation from the original source of this quotation; though I have seen it quoted in English elsewhere, the source of the translation is unclear. Hence my special gratitude to both Ambassador Kurtzer and Leanna Feldman.

3. Chaim Nachman Bialik, quoted in Stuart Schoffman, "Bialik on the Lecture Circuit," *Havruta: A Journal of Jewish Conversation* no. 7 (Summer 2011): 65.

4. Tal Becker, "Beyond Survival: Jewish Values and Aspirational Zionism," *Havruta: A Journal of Jewish Conversation* no. 7 (Summer 2011): 56–63.

Metrics for Measuring Your Life

1. Viktor Frankl, *Man's Search for Meaning* (New York: Simon and Schuster, 1959), 65.

2. This quotation is often attributed to Heschel, but the actual source is unknown.

3. Martin Buber, *Tales of the Chassidim* (New York: Schocken Books, 1947), 251.

4. I am grateful to my friend Dr. Ron Wolfson, who inspired the ideas for the first part of this chapter in his book *The Seven Questions You're Asked in Heaven: Reviewing and Renewing Your Life on Earth* (Woodstock, VT: Jewish Lights, 2009). I have rearranged the questions slightly to reflect the Talmudic order of these ideas.

Redefining Success

1. Viktor Frankl, *Man's Search for Meaning* (Boston: Beacon Press, 2006), preface.

2. Ric Elias, "Three Things I Learned While My Plane Crashed," March 2011, www.ted.com/talks/ric_elias.

3. Elisabeth Kübler-Ross, as quoted in Amy Eilberg, Janet Offel, and Nancy Flam, *Acts of Loving-Kindness: A Training Manual for Bikur Holim* (San Francisco: Bay Area Jewish Healing Center, 1992), 19–20.

4. Walt Whitman, "Song of Myself" (1892); available at www.poetryfoundation.org/poems-and-poets/poems/detail/45477.

5. Rabbi Amy Eilberg, *From Enemy to Friend: Jewish Wisdom and the Pursuit of Peace* (New York: Orbis, 2014), 152.

Creating Your Legacy

1. Henry Wadsworth Longfellow, "A Psalm of Life" (1838), available at www.poetryfoundation.org/poems-and-poets/poems/detail/44644.

2. See Jack Riemer and Nathaniel Stampfer, eds., *Ethical Wills: A Modern Jewish Treasury* (New York: Schocken Books, 1991) and *Ethical Wills and How to Prepare Them: A Guide to Sharing Your Values from Generation to Generation* (Woodstock, VT: Jewish Lights), 2015.

3. Viktor Frankl, *Man's Search for Meaning* (Boston: Beacon Press, 2006). Frankl had written a manuscript on his theory of logotherapy that was lost when the Nazis deported him to the death camps. His desire to rewrite his manuscript was one of the reasons he had the will to survive.

Why Optimism Is Better Than Pessimism

1. This quotation is also often attributed (erroneously it seems) to Churchill. I am unable to confirm the true source, but its wisdom remains, no matter who first spoke the words.

2. Nelson Mandela, *Long Walk to Freedom* (New York: Little, Brown, 2008), eBook edition, section 61.

3. Timothy Elliott, quoted in Daniel Goleman, "Hope Emerges as Key to Success in Life," *New York Times*, December 24, 1991, www.nytimes.com/1991/12/24/science/hope-emerges-as-key-to-success-in-life.html.

4. Abraham Joshua Heschel, quoted in Susannah Heschel, "What Selma Means to the Jews," *Jewish Telegraph Agency*, January 18, 2015, www.jta.org/2015/01/18/news-opinion/opinion/op-ed-what-selma-meant-to-the-jews.

5. *The Autobiography of Martin Luther King, Jr.*, "Letter From a Birmingham Jail," ed. Clayborne Carson (New York: Wartner Books, 1998), 189.

6. Jerome Groopman, *The Anatomy of Hope: How People Prevail in the Face of Illness* (New York: Random House, 2005), xiv.

7. *The Empty Chair—Finding Hope and Joy: Timeless Wisdom from a Hasidic Master, Rebbe Nachman of Breslov*, adapted by Moshe Mykoff and the Breslov Research Institute from *Rabbi Nachman's Wisdom* (Woodstock, VT: Jewish Lights, 1994), 113.

8. Nachshon ben Aminadav is cited in Numbers 1:7 as the chief of the tribe of Judah.

9. Babylonian Talmud, *Sotah* 36a, *Mechilta B'shalach*.

10. Rabbi Richard Levy, "*Dipping into Salty Waters*," J Street Haggadah Supplement (2013), https://s3.amazonaws.com/s3.jstreet.org/images/J_Street_PassoverGuide_Flat_0313.pdf.

Forgiveness

1. Jack Kornfield, *The Art of Forgiveness, Lovingkindness, and Peace* (New York: Bantam Books, 2002), 44–46.

2. Laura Blumenfeld, *Revenge: A Story of Hope* (New York: Simon and Schuster, 2002), 360–64.

3. Eaknath Easwaran, *Gandhi the Man: How One Man Changed Himself to Change the World* (Tomales, CA: Nilgiri Press, 2011), 106.

4. Mahatma Gandhi, *All Men Are Brothers: Autobiographical Reflections*, comp. and ed. Krishna Kipalani (New York: Continuum, 2004).

5. Viktor Frankl, *Man's Search for Meaning* (New York: Simon and Schuster, 1959), 65.

6. Kornfield, *The Art of Forgiveness, Lovingkindness, and Peace*, 22.

7. Michael Lerner, "Forgiveness," *Tikkun Magazine*, May 25, 2010, www.tikkun.org/nextgen/forgiveness.

8. Alden Nolan, "Reflections on Forgiveness," Network for Spiritual Progressives, www.spiritualprogressives.org/article.php/20100524180823527 (accessed March 10, 2017), italics added.

9. Lewis B. Smedes, *Forgive and Forget: Healing the Hurts We Don't Deserve* (New York: HarperCollins, 1996), 152.

Suggestions for Further Reading

Blumenfeld, Laura. *Revenge: A Story of Hope*. New York: Simon and Schuster, 2002.

Eilberg, Amy. *From Enemy to Friend: Jewish Wisdom and the Pursuit of Peace*. New York: Orbis Books, 2014.

Frankl, Viktor. *Man's Search for Meaning*. New York: Simon and Schuster, 1946.

Green, Arthur. *Radical Judaism: Rethinking God and Tradition*. New Haven, CT: Yale University Press, 2010.

Haidt, Jonathan. *The Happiness Hypothesis: Finding Modern Truth in Ancient Wisdom*. New York: Basic Books, 2006.

Hertzberg, Arthur, ed. *The Zionist Idea: A Historical Analysis and Reader*. New York: Atheneum, 1959.

Heschel, Abraham Joshua. *The Earth Is the Lord's* and *The Sabbath*. New York: Harper and Row, 1951.

———. *God in Search of Man: A Philosophy of Judaism*. New York: Harper and Row, 1955.

Sacks, Jonathan. *Not in God's Name: Confronting Religious Violence*. New York: Schocken Books, 2015.

Shapira, Anita. *Israel: A History*. Waltham, MA: Brandeis University Press, 2012.

Shavit, Ari. *My Promised Land: The Triumph and Tragedy of Israel*. New York: Spiegel & Grau, 2013.

Smedes, Lewis B. *The Art of Forgiving: When You Need to Forgive and Don't Know How*. New York: Ballantine Books, 1996.

Steinberg, Milton. *As a Driven Leaf*. New York: Behrman House. 1939.

———. *Basic Judaism*. New York: Harvest, 1947.

Tenzin Gyatso (the Dalai Lama), and Howard C. Cutler. *The Art of Happiness: A Handbook for Living*. New York: Riverhead Books, 1998.